★ ★ 'Ware Sher~~man~~

DATE DUE

~~DE 1 2 00~~			
~~DE 12 00~~			
~~MY 2 0 03~~			
~~ND 9 04~~			
NO 30 04			
~~DE 1 7 08~~			

Joseph LeConte·
From a portrait by Scarborough

'WARE SHERMAN

*A Journal of Three Months'
Personal Experience in
the Last Days of the Confederacy*

Joseph LeConte

★

*With an Introductory Reminiscence
by His Daughter*
Caroline LeConte

*With a New Introduction
by* William Blair

Louisiana State University Press
Baton Rouge

ement with the University of

America

oo   99

Library of Congress Cataloging-in-Publication Data

LeConte, Joseph, 1823–1901.
   'Ware Sherman : a journal of three months personal experience in
the last days of the Confederacy / by Joseph LeConte ; with an introductory reminiscence by his daughter, Caroline LeConte, and a new
introduction by William Blair.
        p.   cm.
   Previously published: Berkeley : University of California Press, 1937.
   Includes index.
   ISBN 0-8071-2395-1 (alk. paper)
   1. LeConte, Joseph, 1823–1901—Diaries.   2. United States—
History—Civil War, 1861–1865—Personal narratives, Confederate.
3. Georgia—History—Civil War, 1861–1865—Social aspects—
Southern States.   5. Sherman's March to the Sea—Personal narratives, Confederate.   6. Scientists—Southern States—Diaries.
7. Liberty County (Ga.)—Biography.   I. Title.
E605.L463   1999
973.7′82—dc21
   [B]   98-50885
                                                              CIP

The paper in this book meets the guidelines for permanence and
durability of the Committee on Production Guidelines for Book
Longevity of the Council on Library Resources. ∞

Contents

Introduction to the 1999 Edition
William Blair

BOOKISH people are generally not thought of as comfortable in the outdoors, but Joseph LeConte hardly fits this stereotype. To the contrary, his intellectual career prepared this famous scientist for enduring inclement weather and other hardships, which ultimately helped him avoid capture by Union soldiers. As a boy he gained relief from chores through exploration of the countryside around his father's plantation. He found similar respite while training as a physician, heading west to investigate the headwaters of the Mississippi River. In the 1850s, six weeks at Key West grew into an important paper on the Gulf Stream's role in the formation of the Florida peninsula. By the time guns fired on Fort Sumter, LeConte already had earned a reputation in the scientific community for his observations of the natural environment. These experiences probably helped the man who would become one of the founding professors at the University of California feel at home in a swamp, casually reading a novel while soldiers from Sherman's army beat the surrounding bushes to take him prisoner.

Such are the adventures that readers will find in 'Ware Sherman, a little book about one person caught in a big war. This work does not engage in large issues or reveal deep truths about life in the South during the conflict. On one level its message is the rather traditional southern assessment of Yankees as brutes, slaves as primarily faithful, and white citizens as reluctant Confederates who turned into unanimous supporters of the Lost Cause. Yet the journal's focus on a single person's enterprise in avoiding Sherman's army can be compelling, especially because of the author's ability as an observer and storyteller. The tale also performs a scholarly service by illustrating the problems of civilians whom fate placed in the way of a voracious enemy—a recent topic of interest for works on the home front. *'Ware Sherman* thus entertains while also providing nuggets of insight useful for historians and lay persons.

LeConte's narrative reveals his adventures on two separate trips: one in late 1864 to bring his daughter from behind enemy lines in Liberty County, Georgia, and another shortly afterward to try to keep government matériel and personal valuables from falling into Union hands. While braving the elements and narrowly eluding capture, LeConte kept a record of his journey on scraps of paper, later polishing the notes into a smoother version. Although he published prolifically—especially a wide range of scientific articles—the manuscript was not printed until thirty-six years after his death, even though its existence was known. A former student, who finished LeConte's autobiography two years after the author died in 1901, filled out the chapters on the war years by excerpting material from LeConte's personal record. The scientist had glossed over his experiences, using only a paragraph to cover his wartime moments.[1] His daughter Caroline eventually helped in the publication of the full account, which came in 1937 through the auspices of LeConte's postwar institution, the University of California.

Before dodging Union soldiers in the swamp, LeConte demonstrated greater promise as a scientist, brushing shoulders with some of the top academicians in America. Born in

1. Joseph LeConte, *The Autobiography of Joseph LeConte,* ed. William Dallam Armes (New York: D. Appleton and Company, 1903), vii.

Liberty County, Georgia, on February 26, 1823, he received little formal training. But if schooling did not run in the family, learning did. Joseph was tutored by none other than Alexander Stephens, the keen-minded man who was made vice-president of the Confederacy. Joseph's older brother, John, also became a noted scientist and eventually president of the University of California. As Joseph entered higher education, he made up for any lack of formal schooling by amassing an impressive pedigree. In 1841, he graduated from Franklin College, University of Georgia, then trained as a doctor at the College of Physicians and Surgeons, New York. For a while he practiced medicine in Macon, Georgia, but found scientific inquiry more to his liking. He entered the Lawrence Scientific School of Harvard, where famed naturalist Louis Agassiz took him under wing. Leaving behind the medical profession, LeConte went wholesale into the study of natural science, which earned him teaching positions at Oglethorpe University, the University of Georgia, and South Carolina College.

As the war came, LeConte had developed strong opinions in the campaign for southern rights. In his autobiography, the scientist portrayed himself as a reluctant Confederate who saw problems with secession but who quickly lost these reservations with the election of Abraham Lincoln. He never explained his transformation in his published account, but he had grown up as part of the planter class and had adopted many of the values of the southern gentry. LeConte himself owned in excess of sixty slaves, who operated his plantation in Georgia. Although he never directly connected the war with slavery, his wartime journal and postwar memoirs reveal him as a wholehearted Confederate.

The Civil War forced LeConte and his colleagues to find other work. At first, South Carolina College tried to stay open, but in the summer of 1862 the institution closed its doors as more and more men were needed in the ranks. Although his salary continued as a state employee, it was not enough to make ends meet. LeConte first performed as an arbiter on whether the Confederate government could possess nitre caves. In 1863 he was asked to serve as a chemist for a Columbia laboratory built to produce medicines for the army. Finally, in 1864, he became a chemist with the Confederate Nitre and Mining Bureau in Columbia, a position he still held when Sherman's men left Atlanta in November and drew the LeConte family personally into the conflict.

The advance of the Union army deep into Georgia had taken a number of Confederate citizens by surprise. LeConte's daughter Sallie, age fourteen, had been visiting with her aunt about thirty-five miles south of Savannah. Few people believed the enemy would penetrate there, at least not from the land side. LeConte's journal opens in early December 1864, as Federal soldiers made their way toward his family. Growing increasingly anxious as word of Sherman's progress filtered into Columbia, LeConte finally left on December 9, 1864, to check on his widowed sister, two nieces, and daughter. The trip quickly turned into a grueling campaign as it became clear that Federal soldiers had arrived. The enemy had burned railroad tracks, forcing LeConte to take an 850-mile detour even though he had been within forty-five miles of his destination. Eventually, he found his daughter and brought her home, but it wasn't until February 7 that the bedraggled scientist arrived in Columbia. His daughter Emma—whose own diary of this time has won a firm place in the literature of the Civil War—noted that he was "wet through and in rags."[2]

2. Emma LeConte, *When the World Ended: The Diary of Emma*

He had little time to rest. On February 15 LeConte received orders to shift the chemical laboratory to Richmond to keep government property from falling into Union hands. Once again he set out to dodge the enemy. Although he avoided capture, the wagons were taken by Union soldiers, costing LeConte not only the government's but also his own property.

Both journeys give readers a glimpse into the home front in the Deep South at this stage of the war. While food was a treasure constantly hunted, LeConte's first sojourn shows that most farmers in this portion of Georgia still had provisions to share, and did so readily with people judged to be friends. The fare was hardly luxurious, and absent were items such as coffee; however, the availability of food reinforces why the Union considered the region one of strategic significance. Georgia farmers had been making the transition from growing cotton to planting more foodstuffs as the Deep South increased in importance as a granary for the Confederacy. Railroads moved these provisions from Georgia through the Carolinas and up to the Army of Northern Virginia at Petersburg. One way to strike at the Confederacy's ability to survive was to deny this precious resource. Because the southern war effort depended on its citizens to produce food for the government, the Union war machine turned toward civilians in an effort to strip the countryside of provisions.

This sensible strategic vision, however, looks less tidy from the ground level. Civilians lived in chaos, raising the anxiety level. No one knew if or when a Union patrol would encounter a farm. There was little sense of where the enemy roamed, or even the direction they might come from. Suddenly, horses

---

LeConte, ed. Earl Schenck Miers, with foreword by Anne Firor Scott (Lincoln: University of Nebraska Press, 1957), 67.

would appear with blue-uniformed riders who began to divest the farm and home of goods. The extent of destruction then seemingly depended upon the whim of the soldiers. Along the way some personal treasure might disappear. Most homes remained standing, but some did not. Under the circumstances, residents could trust no one they did not know personally. Not even men in gray uniforms were safe: Confederate militia sometimes caused as much damage as Union soldiers. It was better to suspect any stranger as a marauder until intentions could be known. Male civilians also presented a threat to the Union soldiers, who could never be sure who might turn into a bushwacker or serve as a Rebel spy. For Sherman's men, it was better to seize a suspicious man and send him off for interrogation than to take a chance he might plan an ambush.

Thus, any hint of the enemy in a neighborhood set up an interesting pattern in which civilian men fled to the nearest woods to protect themselves and the livestock, while women stayed home to encounter the foe. No one at the time seemed to find this arrangement strange. Farms depended upon the labor and management of the household head or overseer, usually a male. It made sense to safeguard that important person. Similarly, guarding livestock was essential because the loss of a horse or mule might make the difference in a family's ability to sustain itself. Yet it is curious that no one thought twice about farmwomen staying to deal with enemy soldiers instead of taking to the woods with their husbands. The wife was equally important in the household economy. Why she could remain home was due to complex reasons but suggests that both sides shared assumptions about gender roles. Most persons did not expect women to be harmed or violated physically. Though there undoubtedly were exceptions, such instances seemed unusual, at least in this particular segment of the Civil War.[3]

Worse things easily could have happened, and sometimes did. When the British entered the Carolina backcountry during the American Revolution, colonial men also took to the woods and left the women behind. But the British strung the women up, stretching their necks until the victims balanced on toes and nearly blacked out before the soldiers let them down. Then the process started all over again in an attempt to make the women reveal the hiding places of loved ones. Confederate militia used the same technique in western North Carolina to try to ferret out Union sympathizers in the mountain community of Shelton Laurel. These kinds of atrocities do not appear in LeConte's account. Despite the destruction that shook civilians, the Union brutality under Sherman had limits. Recognition of this fact might be small solace to a person who has lost most of her farm, but the level of barbarity easily could have sunk to greater depths.

LeConte's narrative also yields an appreciation of the complex relationship of master with slave under these stressful conditions. Time and again in 'Ware Sherman, he praises slaves for their devotion, yet there are signs of tensions underneath. His slaves did help him a great deal during his journey. They did not betray him to the enemy when they had the opportunity, such as when they served as pickets to warn of any approach of soldiers so that LeConte could get a night's rest.

3. I am indebted to Jacqueline Glass Campbell for this analysis. See her *Fear, Fire, and Fortitude: Soldiers and Civilians in Columbia, South Carolina* (Danville, Virginia: Blue and Gray Education Society, forthcoming 1998). Similar ideas form the basis of her dissertation, "'Terrible Has Been the Storm': William T. Sherman and the Women of the Confederacy," ongoing at Duke University.

They helped him find the hiding place in the swamp in which he read a novel while Federal troops searched for him. His slaves also chose to remain on the plantation and continue operations there. However, it strikes LeConte that there might be other reasons for their loyalty than merely good wishes on his behalf. While touched by how the slaves seemed concerned about his welfare, it occurs to him that "they were anxious for us to leave not only for our own safety, but also and perhaps chiefly because they had some of our property which they did not desire or expect to return" (105–6).

In LeConte we can see the contradictory impulses that many scholars have noted in the peculiar institution. To a degree that may seem hard to grasp today, masters continued to rely upon slaves, investing them with a range of responsibilities despite evidence that they might not always cooperate. LeConte seems the most assured when dealing with slaves he knows. Yet he is aware that African Americans served the Union soldiers as spies and informants. He narrowly escapes capture after an African American spots the scientist's campfire and reports to the nearest soldiers. He also decries slaves as helpless in general, despite his having to depend on them not only for safety but also for running his business affairs. After the war LeConte claimed that he never minded losing his slaves, but indicated that the reason had less to do with qualms about the peculiar institution than because he no longer had to care for the people who were, in his eyes, inferior.[4]

African Americans were partly responsible for LeConte's

4. LeConte, *Autobiography*, 232. For more on the complex relations of masters and slaves in Georgia, see Clarence L. Mohr, *On the Threshold of Freedom: Masters and Slaves in Civil War Georgia* (Athens: University of Georgia Press, 1986).

move to California. The college in Columbia reopened its doors in 1866, this time under a new name—the University of South Carolina. LeConte once again served on the faculty. When Radical Reconstruction triumphed in 1867, the enfranchisement of black people followed. Republicans appointed to the Board of Trustees of the university openly espoused admission of black students. LeConte and his brother could not stand this. "The sudden enfranchisement of the negro without qualification," he wrote much later, "was the greatest political crime ever perpetuated by any people, as is now admitted by all thoughtful men."[5] He was extremely receptive when he heard of a new university forming in California. The leadership there wanted faculty representative of the entire country and, unlike many institutions in the North, welcomed former Confederates. He and John decided to try their fortunes on the West Coast and the new institution there. But their position on radical issues reinforces that even scientists, who are expected to be more objective, can wear the blinders of the world in which they are raised.

For the remainder of his life, Joseph LeConte added to his reputation as a geologist and a teacher. He amassed more than sixty articles on a wide range of topics and became especially well versed on mountain formation. His biographer noted that LeConte was known less as a person who blazed new research trails than as a synthesizer who pulled together other work or practiced rudimentary field work. He had reputation enough, but greater acclaim eluded him because he was a little out of step with trends in the academy. While most scholars were leaving behind generalization in favor of specialization, LeConte was a transitional figure who remained with one foot

5. *Ibid.*, 238.

in both worlds. He would not confine himself to one subject, but followed his curiosity. This meant that he covered a breadth of material at the expense of the depth that the scientific community increasingly expected from its top-most researchers. He also was interested in more than facts and loved to ruminate on the philosophy of science. Unlike many of his colleagues, he refused to see religion as giving way to science, attempting throughout his life to show how the two supported each other. For instance, he accepted evolution, but did not see this explanation for human origins as contradicting a religious explanation. Rather, LeConte believed that evolution may have been set in motion and watched over by God.[6] Overall, he earned considerable respect in the scientific community and had a good long career as a professor at the University of California.

Sandwiched between publications ranging from evolution to mountain formations was this little journal of his wartime experiences. When it appeared in 1937, the book won more attention in the popular press than the typical academic outlets. But it did receive a warm welcome from reviewers who recognized the journal's appeal. Although historian Henry Steele Commager wrote that the "little volume" scarcely merited publication in book form, he added: "Yet it is not without either interest or charm." In a similar vein, Stephen Vincent Benét characterized the journal as "vivid, unpretentious, and thoroughly good-tempered." Both reviews welcomed the insight the journal provided into life on the southern home front, and a glimpse into the collapse of an entire civilization.[7] This book also fit snugly with the mood of the main-

6. Lester D. Stephens, *Joseph LeConte: Gentle Prophet of Evolution* (Baton Rouge: Louisiana State University Press, 1982), 178–80, 270.

7. Henry Steele Commager, "The Last Confederate Days," in the

stream nation at the time, in which the south enjoyed a nostalgic resurgence. *Gone with the Wind* was a mere two years away. White people tired of the Depression and problems of industrial America yearned for the seemingly simpler time of an agricultural Eden supposedly filled with happy, faithful slaves and kind masters.

There is no doubt that LeConte remained a steadfast Confederate. In his autobiography, written late in life, he still resented the people who referred to the war as a rebellion. He said that the Confederate States of America constituted "a thoroughly organized government, as much so as the United States." He added: "It was a war between the States, or better still, a war between two nations." He also depicted southerners as being unanimously behind the cause, despite scholarship today that has found contention within the wartime South.[8] The journal supports his view that the people in the regions he visited resolved to support the Confederacy even after Sherman's army had passed through the area, although some began to wonder if their cause could survive such force. As such, the region was different from the mountain areas and portions of the western Piedmont, where weariness set in, especially after it became clear that the reelection of Lincoln guaranteed continued prosecution of the war.

LeConte's own end came in the laboratory in which he had worshiped science and religion for his whole life—the great outdoors. He died on July 6, 1901, while camping with the Sierra Club in Yosemite. Part of his legacy was this little book, which allows a future generation to sample the engaging spirit that moved his students for so many years.

New York Times, May 22, 1938; Stephen Vincent Benét, "A Civil War Journal," in the *Saturday Review of Literature* 17 (February 12, 1938), 10.
    8. LeConte, *Autobiography,* 181.

An Introductory Reminiscence

By Caroline LeConte

AFTER the destruction of Columbia, our family were saved from starvation by our negroes, who foraged about for food. Nobody asked where it had come from—whether begged or stolen. When my father returned from hiding, he walked eighty-five miles to Augusta to get food. Railways, bridges, and rolling stock were wrecked, telegraph lines were down, livestock had been shot. Food then began coming in by the wagonload from outlying districts where the destruction had been less severe. There was no money; commerce went by barter. There were no lamps or candles; one read or sewed by firelight or went about with a torch. Somewhat later, when Lee had surrendered to Grant and bayonets ruled the land, my father found a flatboat on the Congaree River, and asked permission of the Federal commandant at Columbia to take possession of it. This being accorded, he went down to the low country* and brought up supplies to Columbia. Such became his regular job, the city government allowing him a certain quota, which, after dividing with his brother, he used in barter. Colonel Haughton,† commanding at Columbia, was shocked to see him in a battered hat and an old, ragged, cast-off "Yankee" uniform, conducting his flatboat up and down the river. He declared that he had

---

* From early days the piedmont and coastal sections of the State were known colloquially as the "up country" and the "low country."
† Lieut. Col. Nathaniel Haughton, 25th Ohio Vols.; Federal commandant at Columbia after the occupation by Sherman.

received from men of science at the North—particularly from Professor Peirce of Harvard—authority to offer any money needed, without interest and with an indefinite term in which to repay. My father steadfastly refused and continued his humble trade of boatman. In 1866 the College was reopened, ambitiously entitled the University of South Carolina. Salaries were uncertain; estates, ruined; we were very poor. But we had a large pasture behind the house and two good milch cows, Hook and Crook. My mother sold extra milk to the garrison, and we lived by hook or crook. Our faithful negroes cultivated the back lot, and we were accustomed to seeing our dinner dug out of the earth, culled from branch, vine, or hen's nest, or in the form of a headless chicken flouncing over the yard. Sometimes Hook or Crook had a calf, sometimes my father managed to get a sack of rice from his plantation. Our campus home, being in the hospital zone,* had not been burned, and our library was intact. As a child between two and five, my playthings and picture books were illustrated tomes on archaeology and engraved plates of the works of Hesiod, Aeschylus, Sophocles, Shakespeare, Goethe, and so forth. I had a doll: he was up in the University museum; he was the skeleton of a man, beautiful beyond comparison and worthy of all affection.

Lamps and candles had now come back; money, also, in the form of paper, down to the wretched little ten-cent "shin plasters." Yet the people of Columbia were gay. That was the time when fine ladies danced in calico or cheap tarletan and the refreshments at an evening

---

* After the closing of the College in 1862 several of its buildings were occupied as hospitals by the Confederate government.

party consisted of a bucket of ice water. This did not do away with the suffering under a shameless graft. The impoverished State groaned under the tyranny of an all-negro legislature led by two white carpetbaggers. Many Columbians talked of emigration. At that time, as in other parts of the South, colonies were being formed for emigration to South American countries. Such an escape was often considered by the family of Joseph Le-Conte, but our father was loath to leave his native land.

Meanwhile, at the North, the most eminent men of science were working, hand and foot, to obtain positions for the two LeContes, John and Joseph. But in the latter part of the war these brothers had been experts in the manufacture of war supplies for the Confederacy, and now, outside of the ruined South, every academic door was closed against them. My mother was wont to say that my father could not have gotten a position in a primary school.

The clouds darkened. The South Carolina legislature, through its negro board of trustees, was taking the first steps to declare the chairs vacant and to convert the University into a school for illiterate negroes. Now, indeed, emigration was imperative; England, Mexico, Venezuela, Brazil, were all discussed in turn.

Just about this time, Louis Agassiz wrote my father to this effect:—A new University is being started on the Pacific Coast near San Francisco. That is so far away that perhaps there may be less prejudice. You had best apply for positions at once. We will back you with strong letters.

In fact, John W. Dwinelle had entered into the California legislature the bill which created out of the College of California a University, and Governor Haight had signed it. The principal men who now wrote letters or otherwise used their influence in favor of the LeContes were these: Louis Agassiz and James Peirce, of Harvard; Joseph Henry, secretary of the Smithsonian Institution; Dr. Torrey, the botanist; Professor Silliman, of Yale, founder and for many years editor of the *American Journal of Science.*

Another friend of distinction and power was aiding at San Francisco—General Barton S. Alexander. As a captain he had fought through the Mexican War; was promoted to the rank of brigadier general; in the Corps of Engineers was responsible for important fortifications upon the Atlantic Coast; and at the time of his correspondence with my father was engaged on the defense works of San Francisco harbor. Of the "first society" of the 'Sixties, he had his residence in the fashionable "South Park." He already knew the LeContes, having met them, it is possible, in New York at the home of their uncle, Major LeConte, also of the Engineers.

On June 19, 1868, General Alexander wrote to my uncle, John LeConte, concerning some of the Regents. Toward the close of his letter he says of Dwinelle: "He is Republican in politics, and by way of sounding him I mentioned your name and then asked the direct question: 'If, upon examination, Dr. LeConte should be found competent to fill a position in the University, would it be an objection to him in your mind, if you knew he was a Southern man with Southern principles and had taken part in the late rebellion?' He immediately replied;—'Not in the least. I want the South represented in the University. I want professors from all parts of our country. I have no prejudice against any section. If I had been in the South in 1861, I have no doubt but that I would have been in the Southern army. I purposely excluded both religion and politics from the University in the bill under which we are acting, and to prove my convictions, *I* was the man who nominated Mr. Friedlander, a Southern man who believes the South was right, a Democrat and a Jew, to be one of our Regents. No Sir! The politics of Dr. LeConte will never be considered by the Regents when his name comes before them."

"These were his words as nearly as I can recall them. I mention this conversation to show you the liberality of opinions which prevail out here. San Francisco—in fact the whole of California—is thoroughly cosmopolitan. Every country on the globe appears to be represented here, at least every one of the United States and every state of Europe."

General Alexander thought highly of the Regents. Mr. John T. Doyle he characterized as "the brightest mind in the party, and when I say this I say a good deal, for every one of them with whom I am acquainted is a man of fine ability. Several of them are men of great wealth, and they are thoroughly in earnest and determined to put the University upon its legs as soon as possible. . . . Mr. Dwinelle thinks that in five years the available means of the University will amount to $2,-000,000 (in gold). Greenbacks are unknown here except among brokers."

On July 23, my father wrote to John LeConte's wife, telling her of his recent letter to O. P. Fitzgerald, Regent and Chairman of the Committee on Instruction, announcing himself as candidate for the chair of Chemistry and Geology in the University of California. "I fear," he adds, "this chair is not yet vacant, or rather not yet created, but there will be several connected with these sciences if they carry out their scheme, & it is best to be in time."

Heartening word came from Joseph Henry, in Washington, to tell my father of his writing to Mr. Fitzgerald, also, as well as to an old acquaintance,* then living in California, "concerning yourself and your brother, in warm terms as the best man they could obtain in this Country to fill the Chairs of Physics and Cnemistry in the University of California. I have, also, spoken in regard to both of you to the new Secretary of the Senate who is from that Country as well as to some of the members of the House of Representatives and Senate from the West Coast.

"I sincerely hope that your brother and you may secure the appointment, not only on your own account and that of your families, but on account of the new-world, as it were, which is rapidly developing on the Pacific.

"The change, tho' painful, will, I think, be the best for yourselves and your children, and perhaps for the cause of humanity. The South can never again be what it was. New habits, new thoughts and new men will have sway. You would no longer be in unison with the times were you to remain, and, therefore, your energies would be best employed in a new sphere and under new conditions."

On August 4 my father made a "formal application for the Chair of Chemistry and Geology. The chair my

* S. F. Butterworth, a Regent of the University.

brother, John LeConte, wishes, as you are probably aware, is that of Physics or Physics and Astronomy."

On December 2 he received a telegram announcing his election to the "Chair of Geology, etc." At a meeting held two weeks earlier his brother John had been elected to the Chair of Natural Science. Both brothers promptly accepted the positions offered with "sincere gratification." "Nevertheless," adds my father in a personal note, "you will appreciate the sadness which mingles with this gratification—sadness in leaving scenes endeared by early association and successful labour."

While waiting to be informed of the wishes of the Board concerning the time of their removal to California, my uncle John put certain inquiries to General Alexander, who answered him on January 10, 1869:

"The Regents are still debating whether they will go to Oakland next fall or build on their new site. I think they will go to Oakland, take possession of the College of California, and start their University there.

"This is certainly the best thing that they can do as the law now stands. The law you know allows them to go there. Suppose they go to their University grounds. They will be four miles from any place—without buildings, without boarding houses, without anything but bare ground. No butcher, no milkman, no grocer, no doctor, no tailor, no shoemaker, no anybody. No anything within cannon shot of you! You might about as well be on the top of the Sierra Nevada Mountains.

"The truth is the University ought to have been located in this city. Here is to be found *some* of the elements upon which to base an Institution of learning: population, boarding houses, buildings, bakers, tailors.

"Oakland will do, however, and has one advantage over this city—that of climate.

"The Regents are sadly in want of a head—a President of the University. McClellan won't accept and they don't know what to do. [In a previous letter he had written: "They have agreed to invite a gentleman, well known to the whole country (but whose name I am not at liberty to mention at present) to become the President of the University with a salary of $6,000 per year."]

"The President ought to be a business man, as well as a man of learning. It would be better, too, if he had had some experience on this Coast.

"The Institution must be started *de-novo,* and with comparatively small means; though the endowment ought, if well managed, to be sufficient in the future. The Regents have, I think, about $100,000 in ready money. They are to get the proceeds of sales of the new water front of this city. This ought to bring in $100,000 more, perhaps $200,000. When these lots will be sold it is, just as yet, difficult to say; certainly not this week or this month. Perhaps not this year, as there is more or less litigation to be gone through with beforehand.

"Besides this, there is the great prospective endowment—the University lands of the State.

"But these lands are not yet located, surveyed, and sold. Who is to take the lead in this measure unless it be the President of the University? These lands may bring $500,000, or they may bring in a million to the credit of the University, or they may be squandered, depending on the Management.

"Gen. McClellan had all the experience necessary to manage this matter. His services as Vice President of the

Illinois Central R. R. which was 'endowed' in the same way as the University is, were eminently successful in a financial view.

"The questions are, first: where to locate the land, in order that it may become valuable, then what land to sell at once to meet present wants, what to retain? which to sell next year? which the year after? and how and in what manner will you sell?

"There now! I have given you a rough sketch. If no election is made, and you think you would like the Presidency of the University, I advise you to open correspondence with some of the Regents on that subject.

"I doubt if the 'Committee on Instruction' give you authority to do much in the way of purchasing apparatus for your Department, until the question of location is settled. I think they are inclined to be economical until they see their way is clear."

My father had given his resignation to the University of South Carolina, to take effect October 1, 1869. He had written to his sister-in-law: "The action of the *ring-streaked** hastened matters a little. A bill has been introduced by one of the animals,† Sarspartas by name, a negro, the purport of which is to declare the chairs in this University vacant on the 1st. of Oct." But in July, he was still remaining in Columbia "to see what the Trustees will do; will then sell off and pack up"; and "start for California, perhaps August 1st."

The students in the University of South Carolina sent

* The *Charleston Mercury* of February 1, 1868, had referred to the State constitutional convention meeting at Charleston in the preceding month, under carpetbag auspices, as the "Ring-Streaked and Striped Negro" convention. Cf. *Genesis*, 30:35.

† Cf. the biblical story.

very complimentary resolutions to their professor on the breaking up of the session. They also made him a present of a splendid Bible—a "really magnificent one." "I suppose," he comments, "they meant it as an expression of appreciation for my Sunday lectures. It is the only present that I would have accepted. . . ." After coming to California my father shaped the material of these "Sunday lectures" into *Science and Religion,* his first published book.

John LeConte, the first elected member of the faculty of the new University (November 17, 1868), left for California by Panama; Joseph (elected December 1, 1868) waited for the completion of the Overland. By a spectacular coincidence, California's iron road to commerce and culture and her State University, chief conservator of culture, date from the same year. One was finished, the other begun, in 1869. Nobody now living can quite grasp in imagination what the Overland was then, or appreciate to the full the story of the building of that road with incredible difficulty, anxiety, and danger, every mile of it by hand, through appalling wastes and bitter deserts and precipitous heights. It was the longest, the wildest, the most dramatically constructed road of iron in the world. The prairies, still in wild grass, were roamed over by buffaloes and Indians of the scalp-taking variety; the desert sands were uninhabited except by savages and one small Mormon settlement. The flimsy bubble villages that had sprung up overnight beside the ribbon of steel had vanished in a day, leaving but little trace. Frequently the laborer had gone to his work, tools in one hand and rifle in the other; frequently the shack that served the men for shelter was an armed fort; some-

times the advancing ties and rails had to be picketed by
Federal soldiers. Racing at top speed for the gain and
the holding of territory, the Central and Union Pacific
had each flung thousands of men to the battle front.
Numbers had died,—killed, shot or scalped; multitudes
of cattle had perished. But now the prodigious feat that
was to join California, by rapid transit, to the older cul-
tures of the Atlantic and the still older civilizations of
Europe, was accomplished and climaxed by the golden
spike. My father waited only to see that the way was
reasonably safe. Then, not knowing very well what was
before, but dreading that which lay behind, he packed
up his effects.

The day of departure is more vivid to memory than
yesterday: furniture sold and moved out; boxes, trunks,
valises scattered about; friends crowding in to say goodbye; my mother, bonnet on, standing, one foot on a box,
lacing her boot in the greatest excitement,—"Yes, we
are starting right away. Yes, going to the new University
at San Francisco.—California! why, that's where you
pick up gold in the street!" Everyone was looking on in
astonishment. California!—the end of the earth, the
jumping-off place of creation! To most people on the
Atlantic, California was a region of Indians, Vigilantes,
and fights to the death with knife and revolver.

We went by train to New York, my father regretting
that he had no time to see his scientific friends in Washington, Philadelphia, and Boston. Men of science from
father to son, the LeConte family had been, from the
beginning of the eighteenth century, intimately associ-
ated with the cultural circles in the large cities of the
East. In some respects California was to mean exile.

At New York we visited Dr. Lewis A. Sayre, the old teacher, the fond friend, eminent authority on spinal diseases, honored with knighthood by the King of Denmark. From Washington, too late to reach us in New York, came a letter from Joseph Henry. Mr. Henry acknowledged the receipt of "a portfolio of papers relative to a geological map of the United States. It is deeply to be regretted that the great moral commotion that has produced such disastrous effects at the South should have interrupted your labour in regard to the map. It appears, however, to have been the necessary consequence of unstable conditions of the antagonistic civilizations of the North and the South. The former resting on steam and machinery, and the latter on muscular power. The two were incompatible, though it would have been the wiser course to discuss the matter calmly and to have adjusted it by purchase and sale."

For the sums hoped for and not coming to hand, my father had borrowed the wherewithal, and started.

And first came Niagara. Like an ocean of foam and cloud, of cloud rolling up into the sky, of foaming water pouring down out of the clouds, it was the fitting prelude to the epic of gigantic plain and mountain.

It was at Omaha that we took one of the earliest transcontinental trains. There rode with us a guard of Federal soldiers and rifles; for it was rumored that Chief Spotted Tail and his braves might attack that train. Spotted Tail did not materialize. Everybody was glad and I was sorry. A fight between Indians with tails and soldiers with rifles would have been the top cream of existence. Regrettably, the big fight did not pull off: we passed in safety prairies, Rocky Mountains, and long, gray desert. Through the vast empty spaces the train marched along with a sort of epic majesty; counting out dangers ahead, there was nothing to beat but hoof and tire, and at sixteen miles an hour you could almost imagine that you heard the locomotive yawn. The passengers whiled away the time looking out of the window for buffaloes and Indians or talking about gold that is picked up in the street. There was opportunity for geological observation. My father gave some informal talks, while a five-year-old, sprawling in the aisle, drew pictures of Indians, buffaloes, and (perhaps) of gold that is picked up in the street. At last we climbed the Sierra Nevada and the comparative absence of snow-sheds gave to the vision the most magnificent mountain scenery. Donner Lake was passed; and tales were told of men and women who for the sake of California's abundance had starved to death between the frozen lake and the cold stars. The train descended to the plain and entered a little gas-lit city.

It was Sacramento. Everybody got out, because this was the end of the transcontinental line. We were hurried aboard the San Francisco river-boat; made a leisurely journey to the city by the Golden Gate, and spent twenty-four hours at the old Occidental Hotel. Then Dr. John LeConte took us over the Bay to the home of a California millionaire. Charles Webb Howard, away for a year's trip in Europe, had let our two families have, for a mere nominal sum, his furnished house, with menservants, maidservants, and a superb garden. And all those whom we had formerly known by name only, presented themselves in warm human flesh. Regents of the University and their families, substantial men of San

Francisco and Oakland, now gave Joseph LeConte a hearty welcome to the far country.

My father went out for his first walk on Broadway, Oakland's only business street. It was lined with one-story wooden shops. Washington was a residence street. Beyond this and down to the Bay lay meadows and oak forest in which were a few scattered homes of the wealthy. "My child, why are you lagging, why are you examining the sidewalk?" "Papa, where is the gold that people pick up in the street?"

But the gold came. It came with my father's first salary. He beckoned the family into my mother's room. Then pulling out the money, piece by piece he flung it down on the bed. "Gold!" he shouted. "Silver!" he proclaimed. And then throwing up one hand, fingers outspread, and with a thrilling cry: "Money!" The women with cries of delight were fingering the strange-looking yellow and whitish roundels that could buy anything from land and houses to boots and shoes. My father commenced paying back what he had borrowed. Christmas came on apace and with it a huge box of toys. "Why, Papa, I never heard of Santa Claus before! Why didn't Santa Claus come to the little boys and girls in Columbia?" I looked up and wondered why my father's and mother's eyes were filled with tears.

But joy, hope, courage, confidence sprang up in the sparkling California air. Already California had given my parents the best gift of all gifts, in the birth of a son. The University was now established in the campus and buildings of the old College of California and as Acting President, assisted by a committee of Regents, John LeConte had already laid out the courses of study. The date was September, 1869, and the scene, old College Hall. Joseph LeConte was standing behind a table as the first class to enter the University proper approached. Clarence Wetmore stepped forward. Dipping a pen in ink, the Professor handed it to him, saying, "You have the honor to be the first student to register in this institution that is destined to be one of the very greatest in the country."

For two years before going to Berkeley we lived in old "Mansion House." At first one visited the University site in a private carriage, and, if it was spring, admired the bare green hills painted with floral magnificence as though swept by a gigantic brush. North, south, east, west, the prospect ran in flowering field or tasseling oats. But now a lurching omnibus was making regular trips, taking workmen to the grounds. Roads were being constructed, wooden bridges built. The foundations of South Hall (the Agricultural Building) had already been laid. On October 9, 1872, an enthusiastic crowd of two hundred witnessed the laying of the cornerstone. During the following weeks, one after another the iron stanchions swung up into place and stood skeleton-like against sky and cloud. One after another, the courses of brick were laid. It was the first building of that which Louis Agassiz and Joseph Henry had called the "new University upon the Pacific Coast." It is safe to say that, in its big universal idea, it was the only one upon the Pacific from Alaska to Mexico. But before South Hall was finished, the large wooden North Hall was ready, and the first class to enter the University, that of '73, had been graduated in the Assembly Room. The University moved out to Berkeley and took possession of its new quarters. Therefore my father abandoned the old "Mansion House" of the College of California for a cottage in Faculty Glade.

My father found the climate and people of California singularly congenial and stimulating. He accomplished here his best, his monumental work. All his books were published while he was connected with this college, and in fact, it was California that led him to specialize in Mountain Structure and Earthquakes. In 1901 he died peacefully in Yosemite Valley, surrounded by his beloved mountains and their evidences of geological agencies.

When my father first landed in California, he prophesied that its University would be one of the very greatest in the country. It has fulfilled his expectations. Some of its early benefactors dreamed of the University as a link between the thought of the far Occident and that of the far Orient. May we not imagine that this is also coming true? At any rate, for us who are sentimental, it is a buckle of gold and diamonds that unites the two ends of the girdle that Puck put around the earth. But even the most practical man of affairs can hardly fail to observe that in less than seventy, yes in less than fifty years, there has been here a quite remarkable expansion. When the whole nation had been bled white by a great civil war, this is the University for which men put their shoulders to the political wheel and to which the people of young California gave generously. This is the University which, when every worthwhile academic door was closed against them, saved the LeConte brothers from exile to a foreign land. My father never forgot this. He loved the University as a mother loves her child, as a father his son.

The following *Journal* of his experiences during the last days of the Confederacy shows the conditions that drove him to California. Day by day, and upon scraps of paper, he wrote this *Journal*. After he had been under shellfire, and after shooting the dangerous rapids of a river; as a refugee before Sherman's army, he wrote it while hiding in forest, field, and swamp; by sunlight, or by firelight in the cabins of the country people. Immediately after his return to Columbia, he corrected this rough draft and probably enlarged it; and then almost at one sitting and while every event and every hour of his experience was vividly impressed upon his mind, he transferred the whole to a notebook, adding his quaintly morphological and cubistic illustrations. It develops that in flight he had ink with him, perhaps in a screw-top bottle; and a careful examination of his drawings reveals that Major Niernsie, Leitner, and others were his unconscious models. When he returned to Columbia he cut out these sketches from the loose sheets of his rough draft and pasted them into his first handwritten book. Therefore the illustrations in the following *Journal* are actually those of the refugee. They are the solace of his idle hours in hiding.

In 1878, when he was living on a spot now covered by the Faculty Club, he complained that the binding was giving way and the poor Confederate ink fading to such a degree that his *Journal* would soon be illegible. He then bought a good stout blankbook, and transcribed the text, word for word. The final form of this manuscript is a careful and accurate typescript made by Mrs. J. N. Talley, a granddaughter of Joseph LeConte.

The Journal

By Joseph LeConte

HEARING from what I considered good military authority that Sherman would certainly strike the coast at Savannah, and not at Beaufort, as I had previously supposed, and that being short of provisions he would probably ravage the whole coast of Georgia, I started this morning [Dec. 9th, 1864] if possible to reach Savannah before him, intending thence to go out to Liberty County for the purpose of bringing out Sallie and perhaps my sister and her daughters from this threatened region, for I greatly feared the effects on her mind—not to mention other possible dangers—which might result from the presence of the plundering Yankee soldiery.

I arrived, 5 P.M., in Charleston, intending to take the train thence to Savannah in the morning. All the hotels and boarding-houses known to me are in the shelled district and have been abandoned. Temporary boarding-houses I hear have been opened in the upper portion of the city beyond the reach of the shells. I know not where to go for a night's lodging. One of my former pupils of the South Carolina College, Gibson, kindly carried me to a house in that part of the city known as Hamden. Found great difficulty in getting quarters on any terms—the lady was just breaking up with the intention of moving on the morrow to Columbia, running away from the threatened city—everything is already packed up, no lights except in the kitchen and dining-room, no wood or coal except a handful for cooking the necessary food for the family, no fire except in the kitchen. By much entreaty and through the good nature of Madam I however finally got a room and, not willing to intrude on the busy family, remained there in the dark and the cold until supper. Excellent supper, but comfortless and cheerless. The gloom and silence weighed heavily on my spirits and filled me with forebodings. After supper what shall I do? Where shall I go? Even the chairs are all packed up except one apiece for the family. Everybody is busy with arrangements for getting off tomorrow. There was no alternative. I went back to my room and sat in the cold and the dark and finally went to bed to keep warm. And is this Charleston, the Queen City?

I learned at supper that the train from Savannah had not arrived and that great fears were entertained that the road had been captured by a detachment of Yankees from Beaufort. I determined, however, at any risk to make the attempt to reach Savannah on the morrow. (Sherman was even then at Savannah . . .)

Dec. 10th.—An early breakfast of good *coffee* (which I had not tasted for two years), excellent bread and delicious steak put me in better and more hopeful spirits. "Can I get a boy to carry my luggage to the depot?" I briskly inquired. "Impossible, no boy to spare—everybody busy packing up—not far to the depot."

I took my carpet-bag in hand and started, 6 A.M., at a brisk pace. Alas, how silent and desolate seems the beautiful city, the pride of the South! But no time now for gloomy reflections. I must hurry on if I mean to take the train, for it starts at 7 A.M. I walked rapidly—the carpet-bag was heavy—the distance was about two miles. I arrived much heated but in plenty of time, for the train is detained by the bustle and confusion attending suitable preparation for possible attack and did not get off until 9 A.M. Upon inquiry of the knowing ones, army officers &c. on the cars, I learned that it was more than doubtful if the cars would be able to go through to Savannah at all. Grave fears [are entertained] that the road is already in the hands of the enemy near Pocotaligo or else at Coosahatchie, but go on I will at any risk. With this resolution I threw off all thoughts of the future and determined to enjoy the present.

I found many pleasant acquaintances on board the cars, among whom are my old friends Dr. Gibbes* and Major Niernsie† from Columbia. I observe also on board a very beautiful young lady in company with a tall, fine-looking officer. I have certainly seen her before. Yes, now I remember. They came down with me from Columbia yesterday. Upon inquiry I find they are Col. Martin, C.S.A., and his bride. They were married on Thursday the 8th in Columbia. She was, before marriage, Miss Sallie Waldo of Florida, and they are now on their way to her father's home there. The Waldos were formerly from S.C., and she was visiting there when captured by the gallant Colonel. They will accompany me as far as Walthourville, Liberty County, i.e., for my whole journey. She seems very intelligent and refined, and is certainly extremely beautiful—tall and stately, with large black eyes, long black lashes, black brows finely pencilled and arched—a magnificent suit of black hair, fair but pale complexion, regular, clear-cut, almost perfect Gre-

* Dr. Robert W. Gibbes, a physician of Columbia. During the war, he was surgeon general of South Carolina.
† Maj. John R. Niernsie.

cian features, her person simply and tastefully though richly dressed. I must make her acquaintance if I find opportunity. A refined and high-souled woman—a true Southern lady such as she seems—I unspeakably admire and reverence.

We ran very slowly and carefully, reaching Pocotaligo at 5 P.M. Here Dr. Gibbes left us to join the cadets of the Military Academy of Columbia stationed here, among whom is his son Moultrie. He has been ordered here to act as surgeon in case of action. We learned here that the road is still open, but that the Yanks have planted a battery within a half-a-mile of it at Coosahatchie, and amuse themselves by shelling every passing car. We wait patiently until dark and then under cover of night run swiftly and safely by the point of danger, though severely shelled. Beyond this we went on without further danger, and I was fast asleep coiled up on a seat when the stopping of the cars at Hardeeville, ten miles from Savannah, at midnight roused me. I looked out a moment into the dark and solemn pine woods and, huddling down again, fell asleep.

Dec. 11th, Sunday.—Waked up very early and looked out. Hardeeville is nothing but a railroad station with one commissary store-house by the roadside and two or three miserable huts in the pine wood at some distance. It had rained hard all night, but is warm and bright this morning. "Why have we stopped?" Upon inquiry I learned that the engine had been sent on to the Savannah river to learn if the bridge and trestle were still safe. It has not yet returned. It is impossible to say how long we may be detained here, or whether we can go on any further at all. I wash my face in the water of the ditches—it is clear swamp water—on the roadside, and make my toilet by the reflection in the same, but what shall I do for breakfast? I had expected certainly to go through from Columbia to Savannah in two days, and had taken lunch supplies accordingly. My stock is entirely exhausted. I try the commissary store. Shut up—abandoned. I scan the whole country round about to find if possible a potato or a square of hard-tack. There is absolutely nothing. Country very poor—houses all deserted. I return after my fruitless foraging about 9 A.M., gnawing a small piece of hard-tack which by diligent rummaging I found hidden away in the deepest corner of my overcoat pocket. As I entered the cars, the beautiful Mrs. Martin was just opening a basket of provisions containing everything that one could desire—ham—bread—biscuit—crackers—butter—cheese—pickles—cakes—sweetmeats—candies—and her own queenly person seemed born to distribute. I suppose I looked very rueful and perhaps somewhat wolfish; at any rate, Mrs. Martin cordially invited me to join herself and husband at their breakfast. I accepted at once for two good and sufficient reasons. First, I was glad to become acquainted with the charming bride, and second, I was almost famished. The acquaintance thus happily made was delightfully cultivated during the day. I was not wrong in my first impression. She is certainly a charming woman—a fine type of Southern lady. I passed very many pleasant hours in her society and had the use of her basket all day.

But I anticipate. About 12 M. the engine came back bringing word that the Savannah river bridge was already in the hands of the enemy and partly burned, and the Ogeechee river bridge was also burned by our forces on the night of the 9th, and, worst of all, that Savannah was already closely invested by the enemy. It was clearly impossible for us to go through—my way to Liberty County lay over both these bridges. Col. Martin and his bride determined to take private conveyance from Grahamville (a short distance back) to the plantation of Col. Martin's father, which was near by, thence by the same means, crossing the Savannah river at a higher point, to the Gulf Road, which would convey them to Florida. As for me, I must turn back to Charleston and Columbia and thence try to reach Liberty County by Augusta, Macon, Albany, Thomasville and the Gulf Road.* I am within 45 miles of my destination now. I must go 850 miles around to reach it. It was a long, tedious route, but no other was possible. So many, many days before I can reach Sallie. Won't the Yankees be there before me? Oh, that I could get on, forward, backward, any way so I don't waste time here! But we must wait for night, for they say it is impossible any longer to pass Coosahatchie with safety by day.

About 4 P.M., refugees from Savannah and the vicinity began to come in—most of them walking all the way from Screven's ferry, ten miles distant, all of them wearied and panic-stricken. Among them was Dr. D———, a skillful physician and distinguished scientist and a large planter in the vicinity of Savannah. I have known him from my boyhood. He had left everything—absolutely everything, except what could be put into his pocket—to the plundering soldiers and negroes. Poor old man! He seems almost paralyzed and nearly imbe-

* The Savannah, Albany & Gulf Railroad. It ran between Savannah and Thomasville only; transportation between Albany and Thomasville was by stage.

cile. He can scarcely walk and almost had to be carried
into the cars. I soon find, however, that my compassion
is partly at least misplaced, for I observe that he takes
much—I fear far too much—gin and water. Alas, what
a pitiable object, intelligent, cultivated—once wealthy
and influential, but worldly and selfish—therefore now
broken by fear and loss of property, his spirit naked,
shivering, cowering, poor. For such there remains
naught but suicide or drink.

From refugees we learned the Ogeechee bridge is certainly burned. Also that a train containing among many
other respectable citizens R. R. Cuyler, President of the
Road, was captured on the Gulf Road, and, saddest of
all, that Fort McAllister had fallen, having been taken
in the rear by a portion of the Yankee army which crossed
the Ogeechee river above King's bridge, and that planters in the vicinity of Savannah are fleeing in every direction. These sad tales of disaster and plunder on the one
hand and of panic flight on the other fell heavily on my
heart and filled me with forebodings of evil.

About 5 P.M. started back for Charleston. At Grahamville Col. Martin and his beautiful bride left us, and
alas, with them went also the basket. I sent a letter by
them to Sallie, to be mailed at some point on the Gulf
Road, informing her of my plans. (This letter, however,
never reached her.) Major Niernsie, who early yesterday
morning had left us to inspect some defensive works,
joined us at Grahamville. Excellent fellow is the Major,
but hardly a fair exchange for the beautiful bride and
her basket.

Dec. 12th.—Woke up this morning at Coosahatchie
river. We did not pass the point of danger last night as

expected. The train had stopped here in the pine-barrens expecting a train from Charleston—can't go on until it comes—patience, patience! Wind blew a gale all last night. This morning very cold, the coldest I have felt this winter. I had to break the ice in the ditches to find water to wash my face and to drink. What shall I do today for food? We are in the midst of the pine-barrens without a house in sight. Major Niernsie had three pieces of hard-tack, each three inches across, which he generously shared with me. We waited all day at Coosahatchie river with only one very decided sensation, and that was a craving for food. About 4 P.M. the engineer of the expected train arrived on foot. "What is the matter?" His engine in attempting to run the gauntlet at the exposed point had been disabled by a shot through her boiler. The whole train was still standing exposed to the shells of the enemy. Our engine was quickly detached, run down, and brought out the exposed train without injury, though severely shelled. Upon examination we found that the disabled engine had been pierced by a three-inch shell which entered the very centre of the boiler and burst within. The fragments were taken out and examined with keen interest, for we also must pass the same point. The road, it seems, is not visible from the Yankee battery, but they have a lookout at a point where it is visible who gives warning and directs the shelling. But for this the danger would be much greater.

About 9 P.M. we started, the ladies considerably alarmed and *perhaps* some of the gentlemen too. Some of these latter I observe whistle in a very careless and indifferent manner. These I thought rather the most

Our train under fire at Coosahatchie river.

scared. As soon as we started, a rocket went up from the lookout. As we approached the point of danger we increased our speed and shot by like an arrow. In spite of the short time of exposure three or four shells were fired at us. One passed about ten feet above the cars and exploded directly over us, but did no damage.

Took up Dr. Gibbes again at Pocotaligo. Spent the whole night again in the cars moving *slowly,* ah how slowly, towards Charleston, apparently because another train was expected from that place with troops to protect the railroad.

Dec. 13th.—Passed a very cold and uncomfortable night. Woke up within 12 miles of Charleston. The train had stopped. We are waiting for a train from Charleston carrying troops to Pocotaligo and Coosahatchie. Not a mouthful to break our fast upon this morning. The jolly, rosy-faced Major Niernsie looks haggard and disconsolate. No telling when we shall reach Charleston.

Another day without food! Impossible. The Major and myself determine to go out foraging. We walked down the road towards Charleston about a mile. Entered a house a little way off the road which looked comfortable and whose open door seemed to invite us in. We quickly ingratiated ourselves with the mistress, an uneducated woman but somewhat well-to-do, living entirely alone—her husband of course being in the army. In half-an-hour we sat down to an abundant, and to a hungry man a most delicious, breakfast of sausages, hominy, sweet potatoes and cornbread. Ah, how we enjoyed that breakfast. The change produced in the Major was most marvellous. Instead of the shrunken form, the loose and hanging vest, the shambling gait, the pale, shrunken, ill-natured face and lack-lustre eye, we have now "a good portly man i' faith, and a corpulent, of a cheerful look, a pleasing eye and a most noble carriage." Our kind hostess would take no money—we were Confederates as was her husband, that was enough.

On returning to the cars we found considerable hubbub and commotion amongst the passengers. Our engine is *impressed* by a young Lieutenant "clothed in brief authority," to carry troops to Pocotaligo. After urgent remonstrance from myself and Major Niernsie the Lieut. promised to send back the engine from the next station.

This is already the fourth day I have spent on the cars of this miserable road. But there is no help. Orders are positive—the case is urgent—I submit. Many passengers, placing no confidence in the promised return of the engine, started for Charleston on foot. I could not, for I had luggage. About 12 o'clock the engine returned and carried us into Charleston in an hour, taking up the pedestrians on the way, but alas, it was now too late for the P.M. train to Columbia.

Major Niernsie and myself were taken by Dr. Gibbes to the Wayside Home, an eating and lodging house maintained by the ladies of Charleston for disabled soldiers. We had been disabled by starvation. Here we were entertained very hospitably, found pleasant society, and quickly convalesced.

Major Niernsie before and after breakfast.

After dinner I start with Rev. Lieut. James Dunwoody on a walk through the *shelled district* and to examine the defences of Charleston. There is no risk in this as there is at this time a truce for the exchange of prisoners. Many, very many of the houses I observe are struck and badly torn, but the damage is not so great as might have been expected from 18 months of shelling. We roam for many miles through the deserted streets. How silent and desolate is the once beautiful city! The Battery, the beautiful Battery alone shows signs of life, not the bustling life of business, or the gay life of fashion, but the measured tramp of soldiers. All those fine houses looking out upon the noble Bay shut up, deserted, and many of them mutilated by the shells.

I am greatly interested in examining the defences,

particularly the huge air-chambered Blakely rifled guns carrying solid balls of 700 pounds. These ran the blockade. I am also much interested in Lieut. Dunwoody. He is an incessant talker, full of original thoughts, sometimes fanciful notions on all kinds of subjects—theological, military and scientific. He is really a very intelligent and entertaining man.

Dec. 14th.—After a pleasant night's rest at "Wayside Inn" and entire recovery from the effects of starvation and want of sleep, I start this morning with Lieut. Dunwoody for Columbia, where I arrived in due time without any incident worthy of record. It was necessary for me to return to Columbia, though out of my direct way, in order to get money sufficient for the long journey by Thomasville. The next two days I spent in Columbia perfecting my plans and raising money.

Dec. 17th.—Having completed my arrangements I start again. In Augusta, where I was detained over night, I saw St. John,* the chief of the Nitre and Mining Bureau, and had a long talk with him. Received many orders and talked over plans in relation to nitre and mining works which must be carried out on my return, which I hope will be in 2 or 3 weeks. (I was at this time chemist of the Nitre and Mining Bureau.)

Dec. 18th, Sunday.—I took the cars this morning for Mayfield. Dr. D. again on the cars and in much better condition than when last seen. Heard from him sad accounts of the utter ruin of himself and others about Savannah. At Camak met Rev. Dr. Howe of Columbia†

* Col. Isaac M. St. John.

† The Rev. Dr. George Howe, Professor of Biblical Literature in Columbia Theological Seminary (Presbyterian).

just returning from Liberty County. Nothing but sadness. He believed the Yankees had already ravaged the County, but was not sure. He had left on Thursday the 8th—the whole of Walthourville left that day in terrible panic, for there was reliable information that the enemy were approaching and momently expected. He knew nothing of Sister's family (who live ten miles below Walthourville), whether they had fled or not. My anxiety on hearing these tidings was intense. I must hurry on or I shall be again too late.

Arrived at Mayfield 3 P.M. All the railroads in Georgia have been torn up in Sherman's "Grand March." Nearly all the travel through Georgia and all the transportation of Government supplies from south-west Georgia, then the granary of the Confederacy, pass now from Macon to Mayfield by waggon-road. Crowds of passengers of both sexes on their way to Milledgeville, Macon and the south-west are dumped here on the roadside without accommodation and with only two small hacks to carry them on. Of course there is no chance for gentlemen in the presence of so many ladies. But I must get on. In company with several gentlemen I walked on about a mile and a half to a Mr. Whaley's. "Can you furnish us with a conveyance of any kind?" "Impossible! You are welcome to stay at my house and perhaps I can send you on to-morrow." "How far is it to Jim Nisbet's?" (an uncle of my wife's), I asked. "Six miles." "Can't you let me have a horse and buggy? I will send it back immediately." I explained the urgency of my case. "Very good, I will do so." Bidding my companions good evening, I started immediately and reached Mr. Nisbet's about dusk. Took him entirely by surprise, but was greeted with a heartiness so genuine and entertained with a hospitality so refined that I shall never forget the pleasure of that evening. Mr. Nisbet told me many amusing stories of his own and his boys' adventures in escaping with his mules and his house-servants from Sherman's soldiers. Found with him also the Misses Lou and Josephine Wingfield and Alfred Wingfield, relatives of Mrs. Nisbet. Ah, what a delightful holy thing is a refined and loving household! Outside, everywhere only desolation and ruin, but within this sanctuary peace and love and even happiness. Mr. Nisbet thinks it almost certain that the Yankees have ravaged Liberty. He kindly offers to help me on my way by taking me over to Macon in the morning in his buggy.

Dec. 19th–20th.—Had a delightful ride with Mr. Nisbet to Macon, stopping over night in Milledgeville at Mr. Alfred Nisbet's (my wife's father). My fears concerning the condition of things in Liberty were confirmed in Milledgeville and again in Macon. The rumor was that the Yankees had been in Liberty and destroyed everything. What has become of my daughter and my sister's family? This thought distressed me greatly, yet I still hoped, for I could not trace the rumor to any positive source. My many friends in Milledgeville and again in Macon urged me to spend some days with them. I would have been glad to do so at any other time, but not now—I must hurry on.

Dec. 21st. (On this day Savannah was evacuated.)— Early in the morning of the 21st I started for Albany, by rail, and arrived there at 5 P.M. Passed through Andersonville and saw in passing the stockade and prison, but took little notice of it. I never heard of any harshness, much less cruelty, practised there. After a hurried and anxious conversation with Richard Hines, which only increased my fears, I immediately took stage for Thomasville, sixty miles distant. I have never in my life suffered more from cold than on this night. The road was in an awful condition, cut up by Government transportation waggons. The night very dark, excessively cold and the wind blowing a gale. All night I was exposed to this piercing wind in an open hack with no curtains. To make things worse, about four miles from Albany the driver ran the hack off a small bridge into the ditch. All the passengers had to get out, lift the hack out and place it again on the road. We were delayed here an hour, and, what was worse, got our feet soaking wet and had to ride all night in this condition.

About 15 miles from Albany we drove up to a station to change horses. It was now one o'clock at night and bitter cold. We all went into the stable hoping to find a fire to warm our frozen limbs and thaw our almost frozen blood. The stable was attended by an old decrepit negro. He was lying fast asleep on the ground, drawn up to, coiled about—almost hugging—a little fire of pine knots. He was certainly the most singular specimen of humanity I ever saw—scarcely above his ape-like ancestor—extremely old, ugly, knock-kneed, idiotic—his clothes a most inextricable confusion of rags, shreds and patches. He was lying so near the fire to keep his shrivelled body warm that at the moment when we came in his rags were already on fire and he must have been burned to death if we had not arrived just then and awakened him. "Hello, Sambo!" shouted the driver. "Wake up, old boy, don't you see you're on fire? Can't you take care of yourself, you rascal?" "Ugh! Ugh! Mossa" (striking out the fire with his hands), "don't git mad; you know I ain't got no sense." It was literally true, he was but half-witted, and it seemed a cruelty to expect any responsible work from such an one.

Dec. 22nd–23rd.— Almost frozen when we arrived, 8 A.M., at the breakfast house, Mrs. Young's, 16 miles from Thomasville. A huge blazing lightwood fire, however, soon completely restored us—and then such a breakfast, and such an appetite [as] can only be imagined by one who had spent such a night. I considered the breakfast very cheap at five dollars Confederate money, which I paid for it.

Sambo with his clothes afire.

Arrived at Thomasville 2 P.M. and after a hasty dinner I spent the whole afternoon trying in vain to find out whether or not Sister was still in Liberty. The little town fairly swarmed with refugees from Liberty. I met and talked with many friends—all confirmed the complete and wanton destruction of crops and stock of all kinds in the County, but I could hear nothing of Sister's family. They were all from a distant portion of the County. On the next day, however, I saw my old friend and former teacher Mr. Samuel Varnedoe, my sister's nearest neighbour. From him I learned that Sister had made the attempt to leave for Savannah, but too late. She had therefore returned home and probably was still there. (I learned later that this was a mistake. She did not attempt to leave.) Alas, what may my daughter, my sister and her daughters, have suffered—what may they not be suffering even now from armed ruffians! This thought haunted me. I determined to go down the railroad as far as possible, that is, to Doctortown, on the Altamaha river about 26 miles from Sister's house. Beyond this the railroad was all torn up, I hear. There I could better learn the true condition of things in Liberty and either I would send word to them to come out to me, or else I would go to them.

Dec. 24th.—Started 6 A.M. for Doctortown—station No. 6, 55 miles from Savannah and 16 miles from Walthourville, Liberty County. On the cars saw Dr. Way's daughters. They said Sister was certainly still in the County on her plantation. The young ladies stopped on the way, but their brothers Walter and Willie went on with me to Doctortown to join their Companies in camp there. The passenger train went no farther than station No. 7. There we took a freight train used for carrying supplies to the troops, and finally arrived at Doctortown at 6 P.M. Found the town so-called to consist of one frame house and two or three log shanties.

I was introduced by Walter Way to Col. Hood,* commanding the battalion of cavalry at this place, and cordially invited by the Colonel to share his quarters with him. The Col. had his quarters in the only decent house in the place. The whole house was given up to him except one room occupied by the women of the house.

* Lieut. Col. Arthur Hood, 29th Battalion, Georgia Cavalry.

The accommodations, however, were of the roughest and most meagre imaginable. A few logs of lightwood on the ample hearth gave us abundant warmth and light. [When we were] gathered around this hospitable hearth, I at once inquired concerning the condition of things in Liberty. I was told that the Yankees were still there in great numbers, but Col. Hood would be frequently sending scouts into the County from whom I could get reliable information. I determined therefore to remain quietly there at Doctortown until I could get word to my Sister.

After partaking heartily of soldiers' fare we all turned in. Two or three blankets on the floor to lie on, two or three to cover—such was our bed with three in a bed, Col. Hood, Capt. Stamper and myself—hard, very hard, but I soon fell asleep. About 12 o'clock waked up by a party of revellers from the Ga. Militia stationed here. They rushed into the room in wild disorder like so many fiends, calling for Col. Hood and demanding something to drink. Col. Hood assured them he had no liquor. After singing "Joe Bowers" and other comic songs with more spirit than melody, finding that we would not rise, they went off as suddenly as they came and we heard them serenading other parties with what success I do not know. I now remembered for the first time that this was Christmas Eve. With a silent invocation of blessing on my dear ones I turned over to ease my aching bones and quickly dropped off to sleep again.

The troops stationed at this outpost of the Confederate forces are a brigade of militia—"Joe Brown's* Pets"—under Gen. McCay,† a battalion of cavalry under

* Joseph E. Brown, governor of Georgia.
† Brig. Gen. Henry K. McCay.

Col. Hood and fragments of several regiments of Wheeler's cavalry separated from the main body and under the commands of Col. Clinch, Col. Hawkins and Col. Harris—the whole amounting to about one thousand men, nominally under the command of Gen. McCay as the ranking officer. There seems to be, however, but little organization or subordination, for the regulars care little for the militia. There seems also to be much discontent and some desertion among the militia. The regulars have learned to take things as they come—they take no more thought for the morrow than lilies.

Dec. 25th, Christmas, Sunday.—Christmas opened bright and beautiful, but a very anxious day for me. How long will the Yankees remain in Liberty? Will they leave it at all? How can I get my friends out? How long shall I be absent from home? I shall not hear from home at all during my absence, for I told my wife not to write as I could not tell where I should be at any time, and I left my dear little child Carrie just convalescing from a dangerous illness. My official duties in the meantime are neglected. Under all this anxiety and impatience I must remain inactive. This is the hardest of all.

During the day my negro carpenter came to Doctortown from my plantation in Liberty. From him I learned that my Sister and family including Sallie were still in Liberty. He stated, moreover, that all the stock and nearly all the provisions in the whole County were destroyed, nothing being left but human beings; that the houses, not only dwellings of the whites but also cabins of the negroes, were completely pillaged of everything considered of any value. My own loss, he states, is very great but less than many others' on account of the secluded and somewhat inaccessible position of my place. All living animals, even poultry, were killed and much of the corn carried off, but some of the corn and nearly all the rice remain. The negroes [are] all quiet and orderly and he thinks faithful to me, but regular work is necessarily suspended.

After getting all the information I could from Lancaster I gave him a pass and paid his passage to Thomasville, where his wife, a servant of Mr. Sam Varnedoe's, is now living. Lancaster is a shrewd, slippery fellow. I have known him as such all my life. The fact is, he came to Doctortown with the intention of going to Thomasville, but finding me here he begs permission and the passage money. How he expected to get to Thomasville without a pass I cannot imagine.

I find here many young men from Liberty among the soldiers in Hood's cavalry, as well as many old planters, refugees from the violence of the brutal soldiery. These are, of course, old men beyond the age of army service, respectable citizens, and most of them old friends of myself or of my father. Nothing was heard on every side but sad accounts of complete and universal destruction of property. The air was full also of rumors of Confederate soldiers and citizens still skulking in the woods and trying to escape from the County, and of some killed by the Yankees as bushwhackers. The most painful anxiety exists among these refugees concerning their friends who are still in the woods. In the afternoon Major Camp, C.S.A., arrived on foot from Liberty with his negro man Marlboro. He has been in the woods for two weeks, attended all the time by this faithful fellow, who brought him his meals daily. He gives a woeful account of the state of alarm and suffering in the County. Marlboro, having seen his master safe, goes back tomorrow. I immediately wrote a letter to Sister which he promised to deliver. In it I stated that I would come to her as soon as I could do so with safety, and entreated her if possible to come out herself or else to send Sallie out to me.

Dec. 26th–31st.—During the whole week I remained in camp, sometimes in Col. Hood's quarters and sometimes in Gen. McCay's tent. During this week of enforced inaction the dullness and impatience of the days were relieved by the coming of scouts from time to time and the reports which they brought; sometimes by the coming in of negroes from Liberty or from Savannah. The dullness of the long evenings was sometimes relieved by long talks around the camp-fire with Gen. McCay (afterwards Judge McCay), a man of acute and versatile mind, on a great variety of topics—political and social, scientific and philosophic.

I wrote three letters this week to Sister and sent them in by scouts. On the 29th I received a letter from her saying that it was simply impossible for her to leave unless on foot, as there was not a horse nor a vehicle of any kind, nor an ox nor an ox waggon left in the whole County, and begging me by no means to attempt coming to her yet as the Yankees were still swarming in the vicinity of her house, and giving an account of the daily visits of these soldiers, the wholesale pillaging of her house and smashing [of] all of her furniture. They had not, however, been insulting to the persons of the ladies. The negroes still remained kind and respectful. The regular work of the plantation was of course suspended, for even if the negroes desired to, the Yankees would not allow them to work, but the service about the house and yard went on as usual. During this week refugees from Savannah both white and black bring sad tidings of the fall of our seaport. Alas, alas! I had so hoped even against hope that it might hold out.

The scouts who come in from time to time reported the enemy still in the County in small force but apparently about to leave. On Thursday [the] 29th, Major Camp, Capt. Varnedoe and myself finally induced Gen. McCay to send a small number of men with a flag of truce, with instructions to find the Yankees if any in the County, to represent to them the painful position of the ladies and asking them to help us in removing such as desired to leave.

I can never forget the week I spent at Doctortown— the mingled feelings of anxiety and deep sadness which have filled my heart since I have been here is indescribable. Never before have I permitted myself to doubt for a single moment the final success of *our Cause*—our final triumph in this struggle for national life. It seemed to me a wickedness, a sacrilege, to doubt. But the whole of south-west Georgia, both soldiers and citizens, seems in despair. The Georgia militia, taken from their homes and farms and unaccustomed to camp life, are in favor of peace on any terms. News of the fall of Savannah received this week renders the gloom still deeper. Doctortown is full of refugees from Liberty and from Savannah. On every side I see nothing but anxiety, distress and despair. In spite of every effort my mind and opinions are more or less affected by the tone of feeling and opinion which pervades the atmosphere.

In my daily solitary walks I have wrestled in agony with this demon of despair. My anxiety for the safety of my friends and of my daughter, the certain loss of everything I own as property—all, all is swallowed up in the dread of this one great all-including calamity. For four long years the whole heart of the nation has beat for this Cause alone. For this sons, brothers, husbands, fathers have been freely sacrificed; for this earnest agonizing prayers have gone up daily from every church and every family circle. O God! and must it fail at last!

The squad with the flag of truce came in on the evening of Saturday the 31st and stated that they had crossed the Altamaha at Barrington ferry, thence had proceeded to Jonesville, Riceboro, Dorchester, Medway and thence down the Savannah road nearly to the Ogeechee river, thence back by Hinesville and Walthourville to Doctortown, but had seen no Yankees. The enemy, they heard, were at the Ogeechee now, repairing the bridge and causeway. The whole current of feeling was changed in a moment. In great joy I made preparations to go to Liberty early next day. Major Camp, Capt. Varnedoe and myself immediately made arrangements by which we could carry in waggons and at the same time (as it was doubtful if we could get waggons enough at Doctortown) we again urged the flag-of-truce plan of asking help of the Yankees, even if we should have to send as far as Ogeechee. I determined to walk into Liberty at once and prepare our friends, Varnedoe would come a few hours later with the waggons, while Camp would remain to urge forward the flag of truce.

Jan. 1st, 1865, Sunday.—Ah, how many pleasant associations cluster around this day! New Year's, Sunday, my wife's birthday. The day too is so bright and so balmy. I started off on foot with a light heart, a bounding step and joyous anticipations of meeting my loved ones and rescuing them from the scenes of desolation and the dread of further violence. I am free again! Activity after my long suspense is itself glorious. My spirits so long repressed rebound like a released spring. Several young men of Hood's cavalry are going also, but my impatience cannot await their slow preparations; besides, they go on horseback and can easily overtake me. (Which, however, they never did.)

The task I had undertaken was no light one to a man of my student habits of life. The distance to Halifax (my sister's plantation) was about 26 miles. With the exception of the bridge over the Altamaha which was intact, all the bridges and trestles over the many swamps on the way are burned and the swamps are full of water; but I remembered my duck-hunts in boyhood in the swamps of Liberty and laughed to scorn all such difficulties.

With the necessary passports I passed the pickets on the Altamaha bridge and was soon fairly on my journey. One mile more of trestle and embankment brought me to "the lake." This is evidently an old slough, or old river-bed partly silted up but never entirely thrown out and separated from the river except during very low water. The trestle over this was burned, but a picket force was stationed here with a boat to carry passengers over the lake. As I was about to step into the boat someone hailed me by name. Looking up, I at once recognized Audley King, but in such strange guise! I had formerly known him as the pink of gentility, neatness and propriety. He was now roughly and shabbily dressed, very much sunburned and very dirty. He was, moreover, literally armed to the teeth with two navy revolvers and a huge bowie-knife in his belt and a double-barrelled gun on his shoulder. He was the most dangerous and ruffianly-looking person I ever saw, except for his gentle, inoffensive and somewhat alarmed face, and his mild, rather widely expanded blue eyes. "Hello, Doctor, where are you going?" said he. "To Liberty. Where did you come from?" I asked him in return. "Just from Liberty—been in the woods for two weeks—just escaped—aren't you afraid to go into the County?" "No," said I, "scouts just returned report no Yankees in the County." "That's impossible," said he, "I myself have just escaped by the skin of my teeth." "Did you see any Yankees in coming out?" said I. "No, but I heard of them." He then turned to two negro men who had come out with him for confirmation. These said they had seen several Yankees yesterday at Walthourville. These positive statements somewhat staggered me, but I reflected that a man who had been dodging in the woods for two weeks was likely to be demoralized, and that the men seen by the negroes might have been Confederate scouts. I determined to go on at any risk. "You will certainly be taken," said he. "We'll see about that," said I; "I can dodge in the woods, too." I went on; but I determined to be very cautious, for I would not be taken prisoner.

After passing the lake the first difficulty I encountered was the back swamp of the Altamaha about two miles from the lake. The swamp is about half-a-mile wide, flooded two feet deep and the trestle burned. With some difficulty I managed to pass over dry-shod by scrambling over the immense rafts of drift timber collected against the trees just below the trestle. After passing the back swamp I was now entirely beyond our lines and therefore liable to fall in with straggling Yankees if there were any in the County, as seemed not improbable. Audley King's scared face and alarming stories still haunted me. Very naturally, therefore, I wished to avoid observation of any kind, but particularly of negroes who I hear are roaming in large numbers all over the County, and who it is said often act as spies and informers. Perhaps I was still nervous, more so than I liked to admit, as the following incidents show.

Immediately after mounting the embankment again after scrambling over the back swamp, I observed on the road about two miles distant three tall figures standing erect and still and apparently watching me. I gazed awhile, but they remained immovable. On [my] approaching [them] cautiously, they turned out to be nothing more dangerous than three upright boards of the floor of a burned trestle. These had fallen with one end in the water and the other standing up in the suspicious attitude mentioned. I observed the same on approaching every trestle and of course soon learned to disregard them, but did not in the least relax my vigilance. Soon after, I observed the glistening of some object far up the road. It was only a momentary flash, but sufficient to convince me that someone was approaching, though no one was yet visible. It was exactly like the flash of a glistening musket. I turned out of the road into the woods and walked on. Several figures appeared, two or three with muskets on their shoulders, evidently soldiers, but whether friends or foes I could not yet tell. On nearer approach I perceived that they were Confederate soldiers and negroes. "What and whence are you?" asked I. "Confederate scouts returning to Doctortown. The negroes are our servants who desired to go out with us." "Any Yankees in Liberty?" "We have seen none, but heard of them at Medway and Walthourville." One of the negroes carried a tin canister—it was this that flashed so in the sunlight. I left them and went on. I must be still more cautious, for everyone says the enemy are still in the County and in Walthourville. It is now one o'clock, I have walked ten miles. I stop for rest and lunch in a retired and shady place.

Onward again at two P.M. I am approaching Walthourville. I must be still more cautious and vigilant. About 3 P.M. I was again startled. About two miles up the road where the Walthourville station once was, what are those white glistening objects? Surely they seem to be tents. I see distinctly four of them. I strike out into the woods and walk carefully but rapidly towards them. They still look like tents until I came to within two or three hundred yards. Only then did I perceive that they were the remains of small white-washed shanties about the station, the larger buildings having been burned. From this point I walked rapidly but cautiously to Walthourville, about one and a half miles. I meet not a living soul. I pass several pretty white houses, the deserted dwellings of my friends, dotted among the tall pines, but many others I miss and only blackened ruins remain. The sun is setting and the long shadows lie across my pathway. The tall pines wave their tops in the wind and seem to sigh sadly. I too sigh gently as I see these signs of distress.

I had heard that one man, Mr. Cay, was still at home, although his family had all fled. I went straight to Mr. Cay's house and knocked. Every door is double-locked. Every window is closely shut, and the silence of death reigns. Finally after three or four minutes I hear footsteps—then a turning of key and drawing of bolts, and Mr. Cay himself appears with considerable trepidation on his face until he recognizes me. I then, however, receive a warm welcome. He gave me a long account of the distress and suffering of the people and of himself in particular—of the circumstances attending the capture of my cousins Joe and Willie Quarterman and of one of his own sons, David, and of the gallantry and narrow escape amidst a shower of rifle balls of another of his sons, Raymond, on the same occasion. The skirmish had taken place in his own yard and in his presence. In reply to my anxious inquiry he said that he feared there were Yankees still in the County, although he had seen none since Tuesday the 27th. After a hearty supper and a long talk about old friends, Mr. Cay invited me to share his bed with him as there was no other in the house, all the rest having been sent off with the family. I did not hesitate to accept and, having walked today about 17 miles and for a week past having slept on the hard floor or else on the equally hard ground, I soon fell into a deep and dreamless sleep. About twelve o'clock we were awakened by a cautious knocking at the front door. Looking out of the window, Mr. Cay asked, "Who is there?" Answer came, "Confederate soldiers. We want to get warm." "Come in—come in." They were young men from Liberty County whose names were all familiar to me. We soon made a rousing fire. They stood and warmed themselves while they told us their adventures. They had been in the woods two weeks—found it impossible to get out sooner. While in the woods they had been fed by the kindness of a negro man, one of their servants. They were certain that there were Yankees still in the County. They had it from reliable authority that there were large numbers of them at Medway yesterday. (This is about 6 or 7 miles from Walthourville.) This information disturbed me greatly. The young men remained an hour, and then went on to Doctortown. Though filled with anxiety, weariness prevailed and I quickly fell asleep again and slept until daybreak.

Jan. 2nd.—Started again at daybreak. Very cold this morning. Ground frozen hard under my feet. Soon my beard was a mass of ice from the frozen moisture of my breath. Soon, however, the sun rose and the eastern sky was aglow with splendor. The air was bracing, and my physical condition was vigorous. My anxiety for my friends urged me on.

I stepped out rapidly and reached Halifax, my sister's place, in two and a half hours at 9 A.M. I did not meet a living soul on the way. No one apparently yet stirring about the house. I approached unobserved and knocked sharply. Dead silence for some minutes. Then I heard someone shuffling slowly along the hall and mumbling to herself. I knew by the familiar voice that it was the old house-servant Nanny. She unlocked the door, looked at me a moment with a terrified air, and then, uttering a wild scream, seized me by both hands, dragged me along by force, she screaming and I laughing, and never let me go until she had dragged me upstairs to the second floor and to the door of her mistress' room.

Here I met Sister and her two daughters and Sallie, all in their night clothes. Sallie threw herself into my arms and exclaimed, "Oh, Papa! did they let you come?" "Let me come! What do you mean, my daughter?" She immediately burst into tears. She thought I had come by flag of truce, for they had seen the squad sent by Gen. McCay. When they found their mistake, they were all overwhelmed with distress for my danger, for they too believed the Yankees were still in the County.

Then followed the sad recital of their sufferings and losses at the hand of the Yankees. The evidences were on every side. Broken trunks, smashed bureaus, over-turned wardrobes—everything topsy-turvy just as the Yankees had left them. No use to put things in order to be again disturbed. But worse, far worse than all was the mental agony from fear of personal violence and in-sult. The Yankees had entered the house every day for nearly two weeks. Every separate gang ransacked the house afresh, entering every room and taking whatever they desired. The mental suffering of these three ladies and of my child only fourteen years old during these two weeks can never be told. They now laughed heartily at some of the incidents—how Annie had fainted dead away when the Yankees appeared in their bedroom, and the blank astonishment mingled with sincere respect of the offending Yankees. How the silver was saved, though the Yankees threatened to kill the servant-man Billy unless he revealed its place of concealment. How Billy resisted all their threats—how Sister sometimes man-aged the Yankees and sometimes withstood them, and even defied them. Thus they went on reciting the scenes through which they had passed, talking rapidly, sometimes one, then another, then several at once, sometimes laughing, sometimes crying.

As soon as I could get in a word edgewise I told them my reasons for believing that the Yankees had left the County, but at the same time my grave fears that they were returning, or had already returned. If they desired to go out they must do so immediately. The waggons would be here tonight. They must be ready to leave early tomorrow morning. In a moment all was bustle and busy preparation to leave. The young ladies were extremely eager to leave at once. Anything was preferable to a repetition of the dreadful suspense through which they had passed. All would go out with me except Sister. She had much to pack up and was not afraid to remain alone—I would return for her. All was arranged in a few minutes. I immediately sent word to Mrs. Camp, Mrs. Varnedoe and to William Jones that the waggons would be here tonight—they must be ready. William Jones immediately wrote me back that he feared it was too late—that the Yankees were certainly at Medway and at Q. Baker's, evidently on their way to Walthourville. My situation I now perceived was becoming very critical, for it was necessary that I should pass through Walthourville on my way back.

The danger seemed so imminent and the appearance of the Yankees at any minute so probable that we thought it best to station Billy, Sister's servant, and Joshua, my man, on the main road as scouts. About 12 M. Billy came running in, saying the Yankees were even now coming down the road. I immediately dashed out the back door —through the yard—through the negro quarters, the negroes themselves with the greatest anxiety showing me the safest way—and onward into the thick gallberry bushes beyond. After a little while I was informed that it was a false alarm—tramps, not soldiers. A little crestfallen, I returned to the house. In the afternoon I walked over to my own place, about a mile and a half off, to see Calder, the overseer. I received from him a detailed and most doleful account of the losses on my place, and the behaviour of the negroes. Every living thing taken or destroyed, all the horses, the mules, the hogs (of which there were 100 head), cattle, chickens, ducks, every wheeled vehicle, also much corn, but none of the rice or the cotton. The negroes throughout the country he represents as in a state of complete insubordination—no work of any kind done. The Yankees had not only stripped him, Calder, of everything but had personally maltreated him and his family. I have little doubt this is strictly true. They have treated overseers everywhere, I hear, harshly, and the negroes too take the opportunity of showing their dislike. To me and to Sister's family the negroes are extremely kind and considerate, even affectionate. Sister and her family are served as usual, and even more kindly and faithfully than usual.

About 8 P.M., after the trunks were all packed and ready, I got a note by the faithful Marlboro from Varnedoe that the waggons had arrived and were hidden in the swamp near Jonathan Bacon's place, about a mile and a half on the way to Walthourville, but that he dared not come any further for the Yankees were certainly returned to the County and it would be necessary to lie perdu for some time or even perhaps to turn back and escape. There can be no doubt that Varnedoe was in great danger, not only of capture but of his life, for the Yankees have sworn—so the negroes say—that should they catch him they will *"grease their boots with his lard."* Varnedoe is commissary for the Andersonville prison, and is very fat.* He is only absent now on furlough to rescue his family.

What must I do now? It was clearly impossible to go

Sallie and I escaping from Liberty.

out by waggon. I immediately determined to attempt to escape with Sallie on horseback. One of the negroes had an old broken-down Yankee horse, left by the troops as unfit for service, which he offered to lend me for the purpose. I had much difficulty in persuading Sallie to run the risk, but finally, with many tears, she consented. "Quick, then, empty your trunk and leave it. Pack all the most necessary articles in a carpet-bag." By 11 P.M. all was ready. I promised and again promised in the most solemn manner that if possible I would return for the rest. There was little sleep in the house that night for sadness at the approaching separation.

Jan. 3rd.—By daybreak our breakfast was eaten and we were ready to start. Oh, such a sad, sad goodbye! "Don't desert us, dear Uncle Joe," said Annie as she wept

* Obesity was common in his family.

on my shoulder. "Cheer up, dear Annie, and never fear but I shall return. Goodbye and God bless you all." I mounted Sallie on the old horse with the carpet-bag tied behind her. The animal was a mere skeleton and looked as if it could scarcely stand. He had a raw sore on his back as big as my two hands. His groans as Sallie mounted were heartrending. "I am sorry for you, old boy, but I can't help it." Joshua, my man-servant, led the horse and I walked beside.

It was now just full daylight as we left the house and entered the Sandy Run road, which goes westward to Walthourville. Pop! pop! pop! we heard but a little distance off to the north. "You yeddy dat, Mossah?" said Joshua. "Yes, I hear and understand it too." "Dem's de Yankees shootin!" "I know it. We must hurry. Walk up, walk up." The enemy were not more than a half-mile distant, and coming southward towards us on the Savannah and Barrington road, which passes closely Sister's door, while we went westward on the Sandy Run road. In a few minutes they would be at Halifax (a). They had just commenced their morning's work of shooting every hog, cow, duck, turkey or chicken they could see. Sometimes it seemed—unless they shot robins also—as if they fired just to make a noise and to scare bushwhackers. The poppings were so incessant that it was impossible to count them. We hurried on therefore as rapidly as the poor old horse could be pulled along, which however was only a slow walk. The popping became fainter and fainter as we advanced. They are not coming our way. It was indeed a narrow escape.

About sunrise we reach the house of Mr. Harris (b). We were hurrying on by this house when he ran out and stopped us to say that it was simple madness to go on, for the Yankees had camped last night at Walthourville and would certainly this morning come down the very road I was travelling. He urged me to go back. I told

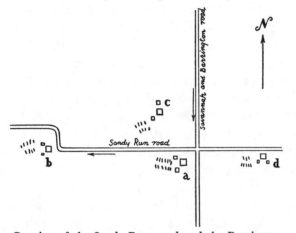

Crossing of the Sandy Run road and the Barrington and Savannah road; *a*, my sister's house; *b*, Harris'; *c*, Varnedoe's; *d*, Wm. Jones.'

him it was impossible because the Yankees already had possession of the road behind me. As I had commenced, I was determined to risk everything and proceed. Onward therefore we went, but with more caution. Poor Sallie! She looks as if she could hardly sit on the horse for terror on my account and her own. We kept a sharp lookout for hiding places in case the Yankees should come in sight. A thick clump of gallberry bushes seems to me now a most beautiful sight to contemplate. Oh, that dark and gloomy swamp! What a lovely prospect! Through these I linger with delight, while through the open pine-barrens I hurry in disgust.

About 9 A.M. we reached Walthourville. We now avoided the road and crept cautiously along the thickly wooded branch (*xx*) which crosses the road at this point, and hid in its skirts at (*a*). Here we tied the horse, sat down to rest and sent Joshua to reconnoitre and bring us word in regard to the situation. We had not been hidden more than 5 or 10 minutes—Joshua had just left—when we discovered by unmistakable noises that the Yankees were encamped in large numbers just on the other side of the branch at (*b*) and not more than 50 yards from the spot where we lay ensconced. They were evidently breaking up camp. In 15 minutes they came galloping frantically by us, within 50 yards, their horses snorting and neighing, and went down the very road we had just come up! If our Rosinante had had the least spark of spirit left—had he once neighed in answer—we would have been lost. But he didn't even prick up his ears or turn his head in that direction—he had evidently seen enough of that sort of thing. Poor Sallie! She was the picture of despair as she exclaimed, "Oh, that I had stayed at Aunt Jane's!" "Courage, my daughter!" said I. "If the Yankees all go down towards Halifax, then we can go on without interruption." It seemed probable that such would indeed be the case. I was cheerful and hopeful, and gradually Sallie became so too.

All day long, Yankee horsemen went galloping and Yankee waggons went rumbling within 50 yards of where we sat concealed. Back and forth, back and forth they went, apparently without definite purpose. What can it mean? When will they go? It was a day of intense anxiety to us two sitting thus alone in the woods. Poor

Sallie! I was sorry for her, but she uttered no word of complaint. About 4 P.M., the galloping having in a measure ceased, I crept on my hands and knees down to the road at (c) and examined the tracks. To my dismay and inexpressible disappointment I found that while the

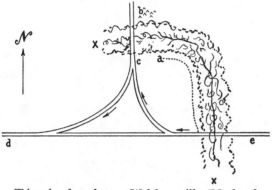

Triangle of roads near Walthourville. (Marks of reference are explained in text.)

larger number of tracks indeed went down the road (e) which we had come, yet a considerable number of tracks both of horses and waggons turned up the other road towards (d), which is the road which leads to Doctortown, and which therefore we must take.

The conviction was thus forced upon me that we could not go on. I might indeed go on by myself without difficulty, but it would be impossible to go on with Sallie. Very reluctantly, therefore, I determined to take Sallie back to her aunt's. I could easily take care of myself in the woods until the Yankees left, and then I would bring her out.

But what had become of Joshua? It was impossible to get along without him. He was our scout, our adviser, our protection in many ways, in a word our guardian angel. The Yankees I know would not hurt him,—he is one of the favored race,—but he had been away all day. Had he been impressed by the Yanks? Or had he deserted us? If so, he will also probably betray us; but away with the unworthy thought! I have known him from boyhood. He has always been faithful and true-hearted. I will not believe him unfaithful now. I really believe he has a sincere devotion to me. But if some misfortune should have befallen him, what shall we do? I strove to conceal my painful anxiety from Sallie under an appearance of cheerfulness. A little after sunset, when everything had become quiet and death-like stillness reigned, we were startled by the crackling of dry leaves under approaching footsteps, and oh, joyful sight! Joshua's glistening teeth and Joshua's black greasy face "made sunshine in a shady place." Joshua's account confirmed in every respect my own observations. The Yankees had some of them gone towards Doctortown. He had been afraid to come back and communicate with us until all the Yankees were gone, lest so doing might betray our place of concealment. He was anxious too, he said, to take time to learn all he could concerning their destination before he returned. He agreed with me that we would have to turn back.

Soon after dark we started on our sad way back. We are going directly into the midst of the enemy, we must be cautious. Soon after leaving Walthourville we met a negro man. He saluted us, scrutinized us closely, but said nothing and passed on. On we went for about five miles. "Stop, Joshua; what is that?" "Where, Mossa?" "Those white things yonder." "I dunno, Mossa, but dey look like Yankee camp." And so they did indeed. They looked exactly like fly tents, about twenty in number in an open place beautiful for camping. Leaving Joshua with Sallie, I crept up with beating heart, expecting every moment to be halted by a sentinel. The suspicious objects turned out to be nothing but a herd of milk-white cows standing perfectly still and leisurely chewing the cud.

Now we are approaching Mr. Harris' house. Leaving Sallie and Joshua in the road I went up to the house to make inquiries. I found the yard all strowed with corn and fodder; evidently the enemy had been there in great numbers and had made free with the provisions. I approached the house very cautiously and knocked gently. After some time of dead silence I heard a window opened above and the demand, "Who's there?" I gave my name and the door was quickly opened. They had already gone to bed although it was but 8 P.M. This is the habit all through the County during the stay of the Yankees— it removes every excuse for coming to the house. Mr. Harris then told me that he had thought that I certainly must have been captured, for I had not been gone from his house this morning more than 15 minutes before the Yankees were there, 700 in number, from the direction of Halifax. These and other parties from Walthourville had been in his yard and using his provisions all day long, and the last had left only a little while ago. How many escapes I have made today! The Col. of the regiment, he said, told him that they would leave the County on Friday the 6th and would not return again. This at least was good news. Mr. Harris also told me that Varnedoe had found the place too hot for him and he would escape with the waggons tonight and return to Doctor-town. The number of Yankee cavalry in the County now, the Colonel told him, was about five thousand.

Silently and swiftly—the old horse makes better speed returning—we continued our march, and reached Hali-fax [at] 9 P.M. Everybody, white and black, gone to bed. Perfect darkness and silence. Knock, knock, knock on the door—not a word or a sound. Knock, knock, knock a little louder on the wall under Sister's window. Pres-ently a whispering within and a head out of the window. "Let us in," I said. "Oh, Joe, is that you? I was so in hopes you had escaped. Do be careful and not make any noise. The Yankees are now in camp at Sam Varnedoe's." The mingled feelings of our friends as expressed to us after we entered can be more easily imagined than described. The Yankees had arrived at Halifax only a few minutes after we left. Our friends had been the whole day in a state of extreme anxiety and suspense, hoping that we had escaped, yet fearing that we were captured. The Yankees who had visited the house during the day told Sister also that they would leave on Friday to return no more. I determined therefore to remain in the woods if necessary until they left and then take my friends out. I would not leave them again. But I am weary with walking 18 miles and still more with anxiety and sus-pense. I must sleep in the house tonight, even though several thousand Yankees are encamped at Sam Varne-doe's only three or four hundred yards distant. I was soon in deep sleep and oblivious of Yankees. Sallie too must be tired, poor child! She has never been on horse-back before.

Jan. 4th.—Took my breakfast this morning by candlelight, and started by daybreak to find a good hiding place. I learned this morning that Billy, Joshua and Davy had been up all night on the roads about the house as scouts, while I peacefully slept. They said that among so many Yankees they feared some of them might have heard of my being in the house. The same faithful and affectionate fellows met me as I came downstairs at daybreak this morning to conduct me to the hiding place which they had previously selected. As I passed through the long street between the negro houses on my way, several of the negro women ran out and offered me freshly roasted potatoes, smoking hot, mealy and sweet. I was touched by their kindness. I was carried by my guides to a strip of very thick swampy ground (Briary Bay swamp) lying between my sister's cornfield and my brother John's place. The advantage of this place, as they explained to me, was that it was surrounded on every side by a deep ten-foot canal, so that cavalry cannot enter it. The Yankees, it is true, are all the time searching through the woods for concealed treasures, or for stock yet unkilled, but they will not go where they would have to dismount. Another advantage was that I could see on every side to [a] considerable distance, but could not be seen. On a dry spot in the middle of this swamp the three boys soon made a comfortable bed of Spanish moss (grey moss). Upon this they spread a blanket and left me about sunrise with the promise to bring my dinner unless the Yankees were too thick to render it safe. As he was leaving, Billy took a book from his pocket and handed it to me, saying he was afraid I would find it lonesome. On opening it, I found it to be an Episcopal Book of Common Prayer. I never knew whether or not he meant it as a joke—but I think not. I believe he really thought (and perhaps he was right) that this was the most suitable and entertaining of books under the circumstances.

About 8 A.M. I saw a squad of Yankees at Sister's house, and soon they were swarming in the fields on both sides of me, popping their rifles at everything they could see, at stray stock of all kinds, stray poultry, wild birds, and sometimes in mere wantonness of sport. About 2 P.M., Billy brought me my dinner. I sent word by him to Sister to send me a novel of some kind, I cared not what, to while away my time. Billy soon returned with one of James' (G. P. R. James), I don't remember which. In the story of this novel I was soon so deeply absorbed that I forgot entirely the presence of the Yankees. The popping of their guns, unless they came very near, did not in the least disturb me.

At dark, Billy again came to me with the assurance that all was now quiet—that the Yankees had all returned to camp. He thought I might safely venture to return to the house. To make it doubly safe, however, he and Joshua would again keep watch upon the roads till midnight. I accordingly returned, Billy carrying my blanket. Then followed the recital of the day's incidents. Squad after squad of Yankees had come to the house, but had found little to take away. Sister and the girls had become accustomed to their presence and no longer feared them, for though rough and noisy they were not insulting. The Yankees had questioned the negroes very closely as to whether anyone was concealed in the house. They had certainly got some inkling of my presence. For greater safety therefore on going to bed I only partly undressed, and placed everything belonging to me, hat, overcoat etc., ready to be taken up at a moment's notice for flight.

Jan. 5th.—Off again to my hiding place in the woods by daybreak. Again kindly offerings of roasted potatoes as I passed the negro cabins. Again all the scenes of yesterday repeated—the Yankees swarming on every side, sometimes within 50 yards of me—pop, pop, pop! all day. What can they find to shoot? I continued to read all day without taking any notice of them, unless they came very near. On returning at night to the house, two or three fires are visible [to me] in the distance. They are evidently burning houses. One of them seems to be in the direction of my place, Syphax, but the negroes say it is Capt. Varnedoe's house or his barn. This is just beyond my place. The negroes tell me that the Yankees will leave tomorrow. The fires are a sign, for they usually leave some remembrance of this kind.

Jan. 6th.—Went to my hiding place as usual this morning. About 11 o'clock A.M., Billy came to me to say that he thought the Yankees were all gone. If so, then the sooner we got off the better. I therefore returned to the house and prepared again to get off with Sallie. The negroes had an old cart which the Yankees had left and which they offered to lend me. We harnessed the old horse to this. This would be easier for Sallie than horseback, and besides she could carry her trunk. For greater safety, while [we were] harnessing the horse one of the negro men was stationed by Billy on the road as picket. Soon the picket came running in, saying that a party of Yankees was coming. I immediately darted off through the negro houses into the gailberry bushes again. After awhile Billy came to me saying that the squad of Yankees had come to the gate, stopped there awhile and after some moments' conversation had turned about and rode off. This incident convinced me that it was not yet safe to attempt to go with Sallie. I therefore returned to my hiding place and spent the rest of the day reading without even the diversion of the popping guns of the Yanks. I returned at night as usual to the house.

Jan. 7th.—Again to my hiding place by daybreak this morning, for I remembered the scare of yesterday. About 9 A.M., Billy came to me with eyes full of news. Col. Hood had come with a flag of truce and waggons to carry out the ladies—he was now at William Jones.' I immediately returned to the house and started off with Billy for William Jones', about a mile off. "There might be still some straggling Yankees about—the flag of truce didn't cover me," so Billy argued. He therefore carried me a circuitous route through the woods instead of by the road as I had first started to go. The fact is, Billy has constituted himself my bodyguard—I know every bush in the vicinity, yet Billy sticks to me even against my will.

Col. Hood seemed greatly surprised to see me. The universal belief in Doctortown was that I had been captured. Varnedoe in returning had stated that it was simply impossible that I could escape; for on Tuesday the 3rd 7 or 8 hundred cavalry were close behind me on the road, while an equal number were camped at Walthourville where I was going and had actually come down the very road I was going up. Col. Hood had therefore made no arrangements whatever for my friends, and was about starting out with Mrs. Camp and her sisters and with Cousin Rosa Screven, William Jones' daughter, and

Cousin Mary Jones, Sam Jones' wife. I felt deeply and expressed strongly my indignation that my friends should have been left out because I was not present, and as they supposed not likely to be present, to press their claims and to demand their inclusion in the arrangements for flight. I reminded him that it was *I* who came first to Doctortown to bring out friends—that *I* was the first and most active in getting up the waggons and urging the flag of truce—that *I* had suffered more than all of them in the attempt to relieve my friends. He finally promised me that if I would find the waggon he would furnish the horses of his dismounted cavalrymen.

With the assistance of the indefatigable Billy I soon got a waggon which had been hidden from Yankee eyes in the thick woods by the negroes. This was added to the others, the horses of the dismounted soldiers were harnessed thereto, and all the waggons filled with trunks. On these the married ladies sat, while the young ladies walked with the dismounted soldiers. Sallie and her cousins Annie and Ada went with the waggons, though not on them, for they all walked. Joshua, my man, volunteered to go with them to wait on them,—God bless him for his kindness,—for I could not under the circumstances require it of him. Sister could not go with them, for the waggons were already heavily laden and she had much baggage. I would come back for her. I was not just ready to go yet, for I wished to go to my place—I would overtake them at Walthourville tonight.

Sister and myself therefore stood in the road and watched them as they went off at 12 M.—nine ladies besides children and servants. It was a strange, sad, never-to-be-forgotten sight—so many ladies who had never

known want or even hardship, nurtured in tenderness
and plenty, now driven from their homes they hardly
knew whither. And yet so great has been the distress of
mind and even terror for the last three weeks that they
are now in the highest spirits.

"Goodbye, goodbye!" said I, "I will meet you again
tonight." A large crowd of negroes, 50 to 100, had gathered in the road to bid them goodbye. "Goodbye, goodbye, goodbye Missie, and God bless you!" was heard on
every side as the waggons slowly moved off. Sister and
myself remained in the road gazing after the receding
pilgrims until they were out of sight, then returned
slowly and sadly to the house.

For myself, before leaving the County I must see Calder the overseer and give him some directions. I went
over to my place therefore for that purpose, and gave
such directions for the year as I thought were suitable
under the anomalous condition of things now existing
in the County.

I returned to Halifax with the intention of starting
off about 4 P.M. so as to reach Walthourville about dark,
but when I was ready and about to start I received word
from Sam Jones begging me to delay until night and he
would join me. He has been in bed desperately sick during the whole time the Yankees were in the County. For
this reason only they did not take him off as prisoner,
though a Confederate soldier. About dark I bade Sister
goodbye with many assurances of my return for her,
shook hands with all the negroes as they came running
out of their cabins to bid me goodbye, and joined Sam
in the road. Sam was still very weak and emaciated from
his long sickness and still very much afraid we may meet

straggling Yankees. This is his reason for desiring to go off by night. Poor fellow, he has suffered so much, no wonder he is unreasonably fearful. As he was too weak to walk so far he was mounted on an old club-footed mule, literally useless and therefore not taken by the Yanks.

Sam Jones riding, I behind urging on the mule.

The old mule hobbled along painfully at a very slow rate. Hampton, a negro man belonging to my brother John, walked in front carrying a large roll of blankets on which Sam must sleep tonight, while I walked behind urging on the mule by beating and goading with a sharp stick sharpened for the purpose. We went on in this way for about three or four miles, when the mule positively refused to go any farther. I argued the matter with him by beating and punching until my arms were sore, but he would not be persuaded. We therefore took off the saddle and bridle, hid them in a thick clump of gallberry bushes by the roadside, instructed Hampton to take them back to William Jones' on his return, and then turned the mule loose. There were six miles yet to go. Feeble as Sam was, it seemed impossible that he could walk so far, but there was no alternative; so on we trudged, slowly but steadily. When at last we reached

Walthourville, about 10 P.M., Sam could hardly put one foot before the other.

On arriving we found that the ladies had reached the village but a little while before us, having been detained by the breaking down of one of the waggons on the road. They were now quartered in an empty house belonging to Mr. McCullough, the family having all fled over the line. All was now bustle and preparation for supper and sleeping. Some were eating cold supper, some were cooking bacon and hominy, some laying down bedding, some washing face and hands, some combing and dressing hair,—all talking, some laughing,—babies squalling, nurses scolding &c., &c. From this stunning din I was glad to escape, so after eating [a] cold supper I went to Cay's, about a mile off, and took a bed with him.

Jan. 8th, Sunday.—Started again this morning from Mr. Cay's by daybreak. Called at McCullough's, though much out of my way, to see how the ladies were getting on. Found them all up and making preparations for starting. They had slept pretty well, considering that they lay on the bare floor with only blankets under them. I left them to finish their preparations while I went on ahead to prepare for their reception at Doctortown. It was a delightful, a glorious morning. I was buoyant with the success of my attempt to rescue my friends. I stepped out with vigor. As I passed the goose-ponds the trumpet notes of the whooping-cranes as they rose from their roosting places were really musical to my ears. What pleasant associations of early boyhood they recall! Without further adventure except wading nearly waist-deep through the back swamp, which had greatly risen since I passed a week ago, I reached Doctortown about 2 P.M.

Here, with the assistance of Major Camp and Mallard Cassels, I immediately set to work making preparations before the waggons arrived for getting the baggage from the back swamp to Doctortown, a distance of four miles. For this purpose we got the use of two pole-cars. These we carried to the lake before night.

Jan. 9th.—Leaving one pole-car at the lake, with infinite labor and difficulty we succeeded this morning in carrying the other across the lake in the boat. In taking it out of the boat on the other side it fell into the water about two feet deep. From this position we four of us (and one, Major Camp, with only one arm) had to lift it bodily and carry it up an embankment twenty feet high to place it on the track. The weight was at least 6 to 8 hundred pounds. We succeeded, however, and then quickly poled the car to the back swamp. The Altamaha has risen so much during my absence that it is no longer possible to cross the back swamp on drift timber as I did on the 1st. In anticipation of this difficulty Gen. McCay had had a small flat built to carry the ladies and baggage across.

The ladies arrived at the back swamp about 9 A.M. We were ready for them. Ladies and baggage were carried over the back swamp on the flat, then the baggage up the embankment on the shoulders of the gentlemen, placed on the pole-car and poled to the lake, the ladies meanwhile walking; then the ladies and baggage across the lake in the boat; then baggage again up the embankment on the shoulders to the second pole-car, and poled to Doctortown, the ladies again walking. All safe in Doctortown by 2 P.M.

The ladies give an amusing account of their own adventures on the way. On yesterday, the 8th, they had made but 10 miles, and camped for the night on the other side of the back swamp. Most of them had to walk the whole way, as they had many difficulties with the overloaded waggons. The most important of these occurred at Jones' swamp. I had crossed this swamp on the railroad trestle, but the waggons of course must go by the waggon-road. The water in the road is now at least three feet deep for a distance of a hundred yards or more. The ladies were compelled to get into the already overloaded waggons. One of the waggons stalled in the deepest part of the swamp. What was to be done? Lieutenant Campbell of the truce party (as true-hearted a gentleman and soldier as ever lived) took out one of the waggon-horses, mounted him and took out the ladies one by one. This gave rise of course to much merriment and many jokes. The young ladies were of course very much frightened and grasped the Lieutenant in a somewhat too affectionate manner. In their terror some of them called out "Hold me tight!" and of course he did. Last of all the gallant officer took Rosa's little infant over. The anxiety of the young mother, the tenderness of the gallant soldier, and the unconscious innocence of the little one formed together a really touching picture. After the ladies were all safely over, the young men jumped in the water above their waists, took hold of pole and wheels, and drew out the waggon. About sunset they reached the back swamp, stopped and made camp. The young men quickly made a sort of booth of boughs of trees, under which the ladies slept comfortably enough after their fatigue, with only a blanket between them and the bare ground. When they got to

Doctortown their provisions were completely exhausted. It was impossible to get anything here but hard-tack, and upon this therefore they made a scanty dinner and supper, and finally went hungry to bed on the bare floor.

Jan. 10th.—The ladies all look haggard and faint with hunger and fatigue this morning. I *must* get something better than hard-tack for them to eat. I went to Col. Hood and represented their condition. He had nothing but salt meat and hard-tack. He immediately issued rations for several days of these, but I must get something more savory. I went out foraging. Hearing of their distress, Audley King, that dangerous-looking fellow, generously gave me a quarter of delicious pork. I did not inquire too strictly where he had gotten it, although I remembered his double-barrelled gun, his two navy revolvers and his bowie-knives—weapons fatal alike to straggling Yankees and errant pigs. With these materials I soon cooked a breakfast fit for a king. I never saw ladies eat so. The fragrance of broiled pork was voted far superior to attar of roses, and hard-tack sopped in gravy was declared preferable to ice-cream. The almost miraculous change in their appearance was like the breaking of a beautiful day. As piece after piece of

Crossing Jones' swamp.

reeking, steaming pork disappeared as if by magic, the dull eye begins to lighten and the pale cheek to tinge, until the whole countenance is radiant with light and brilliant with colour.

Col. Hood promised that he would return to Liberty tomorrow and bring out Sister and some other ladies. After making this arrangement, I started, 2 P.M., with the ladies on a freight train for Thomasville. About 4 P.M. we arrived at Number 7, and awaited the arrival of a regular passenger train from Thomasville which was due at 5 P.M. but did not arrive till 7 P.M. While waiting here, several of the ladies including my own party went to a small cabin in the pine woods close by. Here we found quite respectable people, refugees from Savannah. They really seemed to sympathize deeply with us and were exceedingly kind. They immediately set to work and prepared for us a nice supper, which we would have enjoyed greatly, but just as we were about to sit down the car whistle blew. We gathered up what we could in our hands, bade our kind hostess goodbye and ran for the cars, and off we go again. The road is so unsafe for want of repairs that it is deemed imprudent to run over some portions of it at night. The train therefore stopped all night [at] Thibeauville. We slept as best we could on the seats of the car. During the night a box of provisions sent by some loving mother to her boys in camp was kindly given by one of the aforesaid boys, who was returning from furlough, to the ladies. The box was full of everything nice—chicken, ham, sausages, pickles, sweetmeats, bread &c., &c. Everyone was hungry, for the pig had been quickly demolished and only salt beef and hard-tack remained. But our own individual party got little of the contents of the box. They are not good at the *Game of Grab.* Alas! distress brings out selfishness as well as kindness.

Jan. 11th.—Again a most uncomfortable night. I went on early this morning, purchased some provisions in Thibeauville, started a fire by the roadside and with the assistance of some of the ladies and the negro servants soon cooked a nice breakfast for our party, of boiled rice, cornbread and roasted sweet potatoes. Of this we all partook heartily, felt better and took a more cheerful view of things. We did not get off till 10 A.M. I found in the conductor, Mr. Merrill, an old acquaintance and pupil of mine. He had, also, married Miss Ann Hall, an acquaintance of my wife. Mr. Merrill was very attentive to us. He took a special fancy to Sallie and urged her to go to his house in Thomasville. As our party was large, she at once accepted. The rest of us, namely, Annie, Ada, Rosa, Mary, Sam and myself, went to the house of Mrs. Hayes, Mary's mother. We took her entirely by surprise, but received the heartiest of welcomes. It was 6 P.M. when we reached Thomasville.

Jan. 12th–13th.—Spent the next two days in many fruitless attempts to get my party off to Macon, while I went back to Doctortown and Liberty for Sister. The stage was far too expensive for so large a party, and all my efforts to hire a waggon were unsuccessful. Finally Mr. Gignilliat, an old friend and college mate of mine, as true a Southern gentleman as ever lived and himself a refugee from the Coast, hearing of my situation generously offered to lend me his waggon, mules and driver. The waggon &c. arrived in Thomasville (for Mr. G. lives a little out of town) on the night of the 13th. I made all arrangements for the party to leave on the morrow for Macon under charge of Capt. Varnedoe, who was going back to his post at Andersonville, while I would go back to Doctortown.

Jan. 14th.—Bidding my friends goodbye, and charging Varnedoe concerning their safety, I started again this morning at 6 A.M. for Doctortown, where I arrived in the afternoon without adventure. I found that Col. Hood had left for Liberty only yesterday the 13th instead of the 11th as he had promised. I was told also that he would probably have to go to Ogeechee or even to Savannah to arrange with the Yankees for waggons. If so, he cannot return under a week. What am I to do in the meantime? Must I remain idle here a week? I can't endure it—anything but inactivity. I will start again immediately for Liberty on foot. Action will at least cool my burning impatience.

Jan. 15th, Sunday.—Sunday it seems is a favorite day with me for beginning an enterprise. Sunday I went first to Liberty, Sunday I returned to Doctortown and Sunday I now start again for Liberty. On reaching the back swamp, to my dismay I found the water far more swollen than I had yet seen it. Not only is the drift timber all afloat, but the water for more than a half-mile over waist-deep, and the current very swift. It was of no use to deliberate,—I would not turn back,—so in I plunged, and waded across though it required some severe struggling with the current. With the other trestles I found little difficulty. I walked rapidly and was pretty nearly dry when I reached Mr. Cay's in Walthourville about 4 P.M.

Jan. 16th.—By daybreak I was off again, and reached

Halifax to breakfast at 9 A.M. I found here that I had been misinformed as to Col. Hood's intentions. He would not go to Ogeechee or Savannah, but would be here at Halifax tomorrow. In any case it was well I came, for on looking at Sister's baggage I saw at a glance that Col. Hood would never be able to take it all in his waggon if he had anybody else besides Sister to carry out, as I hear he has. I determined therefore to take the greater part in the cart mentioned before, with the old Yankee horse. The rest could come with Col. Hood.

After breakfast I walked on to my plantation to see and talk to the negroes. The negro houses are about two and a half miles from Sister's house. On the way I stopped to see Calder. I gave him directions to sell at a low price or even to give away if necessary any surplus provisions on my place to such as were in want or completely destitute. I had fared much better than most planters. My place is somewhat inaccessible for waggons, and the Yankees only took away provisions on horseback. There was still, therefore, abundance of corn and rice, although the stock was all destroyed.

On reaching my place I called up all the negroes, and as they stood bare-headed in a semi-circle about me, gave them a long talk. I first asked them if they desired to go with me, or preferred remaining. If they desired to go I would make some kind of provision for them if it took my last dollar, but I did not know how I could provide. If they preferred remaining I had provisions aplenty, although no meat. With one accord they replied that if I had a place to put them on where they would not again be disturbed by Yankees, and provisions and meat to feed them, they would go willingly, but they preferred remaining where they were rather than be carried they knew not whither. I told them I believed they had decided wisely. I next spoke to them of the absolute necessity not only of work, but of organized work, and explained to them that this was impossible without a *head* to direct. They immediately replied that they would gladly work exactly as they had always worked if I would take charge and direct, but they could not get along with Calder. In fact they seemed to think their day of deliverance from overseers was come. I then told them that Uncle William Jones would direct their labour, as it was impossible for me to remain. To this they cheerfully consented. They then came forward one by one to shake hands and take leave. With many expressions of kindness and affection they bade me goodbye. With one accord they said, "We nebber leabe you, Mossa, to go to de Yankee nor any way. If we in trouble we send for you or come to you, for you is our Mossa." I then asked for a volunteer to go with me to Doctortown, pledging myself that I would send him back immediately. Henry instantly offered to go. "Get ready, then," said I, "and be at Halifax at three o'clock."

I then went from my place to Uncle William Jones', about a mile distant, to bid him and Aunt Mary goodbye and to tell him of the arrangement I had made with my negroes. As I approached the house it was amusing and yet so sad to see how suspiciously I was watched through half-opened doors and cracks of windows, and then the sudden change to warmest welcome when I was recognized. I begged Uncle to take charge of my plantation and direct the labour, as I knew the negroes loved and respected him and I believed he was one of the very few who intended to remain in the County. He cheerfully consented. I bade them both a sad goodbye, and again was off for Halifax.

Arrived there I hastily ate my dinner, packed the cart and, Henry being prompt to time, got off about 4 P.M. The cart was heavily loaded with four large trunks. Two of them weighed 300 pounds apiece. The extremely meagre, poverty-stricken appearance of the old horse made me very doubtful about success in getting through. I expected, however, only to go ten miles tonight to Cay's. I hoped to get there by 9 P.M. easily. Billy went with us about a mile on the way to see how the old horse would perform. On taking leave of me, he said (and was evidently anxious that I should believe him) that he would follow his Mistress anywhere and everywhere, even if he had to leave his own wife and children, but that his Mistress desired him to stay and take care of the house. We then parted with deep feeling on both sides. May God bless the faithful fellow!

The old horse worked famously. We reached the causeway (a horrible piece of stiff blue-clay road about half-a-mile long and four miles from Halifax) about sunset. We congratulated ourselves that we had reached this notorious place before dark, but our self-congratulation was premature, for here our troubles began. The old horse pulled admirably, but the work was beyond his strength—at almost every step we had to take hold of the wheels and help the faithful animal with all our might. At least a half-a-dozen times the wheels sank to the hubs in the stiff mud and the trunks had to be lifted out of the cart, carried to firmer ground on the shoulders, the cart drawn out by united strength of man and beast, and again reloaded. Then the hame-string broke and was mended. Then the hames itself snapped. Then the trace broke. The night too was dark as pitch, but for every new difficulty there was a new contrivance. Henry worked like a Trojan. It was well he was a very powerful man, or we never could have accomplished the task. We were three full hours getting over the half-mile of causeway. We got over at last, but the old horse was so strained that he was no longer fit for service. Even on good roads he got on now with difficulty.

We got to the skirts of Walthourville about 11 P.M. "Now push on for Cay's." Alas, as soon as we struck the deep sand characteristic of this place, the old horse came to a dead stop and neither force nor persuasion could stir him. We again took out all the trunks, but all to no purpose. He was completely broken down, and had made up his mind he would die rather than go any further. What was to be done? It was yet a mile to Cay's. It was plain we could not get there.

I sent Henry to get the assistance of Sam,—a negro man belonging to Mrs. Handley, whose cabin we had just passed about a hundred yards back,—with Sam's assistance we got the horse and cart to Mrs. Handley's lot (the house is now of course deserted), and then took the trunks on our shoulders to the same place, where we got fairly settled about midnight.

Sam was really kind and attentive to me and that without the least expectation of any personal benefit. He carried me to his cabin, made a rousing fire, spread for me a mattress and a pair of blankets before the fire for my bed. I ate a hearty supper of cold meats which I had brought in my pocket, lay down before the fire and was soon in a sound sleep. Indeed I needed it, for I had been on my feet constantly from six in the morning until midnight, I had walked at least 25 miles and for the last eight hours I had been straining my muscles to the extent of their powers.

I must not miss this opportunity of paying a tribute to the blacks. Closest association doesn't destroy their sincere homage to the white gentleman, an homage only equalled by the old-time homage to the nobility.

Jan. 17th.—The violent muscular straining of yesterday makes me a little stiff and sore this morning. After an early and hearty breakfast of cold meats supplemented by Sam with hot cornbread and roasted potatoes, and after a trifling present to Sam, which I had to press on him, we are off again and I soon active and supple as ever. After going about a mile I was greatly startled by the apparition of about a dozen horses tied to the palings of a house within 200 yards of the road and only open pine-barren between. A careful reconnoitring, however, revealed the fact that they were Confederates, not Yankee horsemen. Onwards then we hastened.

By the road I was now following we do not strike the railroad until we reach Johnson's station, No. 5. We have therefore 8 or 10 miles of pine-barren road. The open pine-barrens in this region are intersected in every direction by roads which seem about equally plain. When near the goose-ponds we missed the way. After much delay and much useless straining of the old horse in heavy sand, we cut across the pine-barrens and recovered the direct road. On account of this delay we did not reach Johnson's station until 3 P.M. The horse is completely used up. The awful Jones' swamp of which the ladies gave such dreadful accounts is still before us. It is clearly impossible for the old horse to take us to Doctortown tonight; he must rest.

In this dilemma I determined to leave Henry here with the cart and horse while I hurry on to Doctortown to return tomorrow with a good strong mule. Following down the railroad, I reached the back swamp about sunset; having heard at Johnson's that there was a ferry a few hundred yards down the swamp, rather than wade across again I went down to this point. I found there a small canoe in use by Mallard Cassels to carry over household effects of all kinds with the intention of moving to Thomasville, as his father and whole family are abandoning Liberty. After some delay I got a place as passenger in the canoe, along with a barrel of molasses as freight and a negro man as engineer. The cask was not properly secured. I was already in and seated; as the negro man got in, the canoe tilted a little, the cask rolled from one side to the other, upset the canoe, and spilled the whole contents, human and saccharine, into the water about waist-deep. I saw at once that it would take some time to raise and bail out the canoe. I was thoroughly wet already. I had no time to spare. Leaving them therefore to recover the barrel and canoe as best they could, I turned back to the trestle and waded across the swamp at the usual place. It was pitch-dark. I stumbled about in the water more than waist-deep for half a mile, but passed over in safety.

An hour more of rapid walking brought me to Doctortown. Went immediately to Gen. McCay's quarters. Supper just ready—ate heartily—then stood awhile before a blazing fire steaming and drying, but becoming extremely sleepy I didn't wait to complete the process but tumbled into bed with my clothes still very wet, and slept soundly.

Jan. 18th.—After early breakfast, I looked over the mules in charge of Col. Hood with a view to selection. Poor, miserable, emaciated creatures, all of them. The only one which seemed at all fit for service was a very small animal, too light I feared to bring the cart over Jones's swamp and still worse over [the] back swamp. But there being no alternative, I took this one. Having no saddle, I sometimes led him and sometimes bestrode him on a folded blanket. This obstinate little mule gave me much trouble, indeed far more than he was worth. You shall judge. First, at the lake he would not get into the boat. We tried to put him in by force, but in vain. Finally we fairly lifted him off his feet, pushed him into the water, dragged him into the deep water, and forced him to swim over behind the boat. Again, at [the] back-swamp ferry I undertook to lead him over behind a cart which Cassels was about to drive over, I of course sitting in the cart. The mule was secured by a strong rope which I held in my hand. The water was deep—swimming deep for the little mule [and] he remembered his experience at the lake. The horse in the cart was spirited and somewhat alarmed, and therefore plunged along rapidly and unequally. The mule was unwilling to lead, I was unwilling to let go the rope, the rope was unwilling to break; the consequence of all this concatenation of unwillingness was that I was pulled out of the cart into the water nearly up to my neck. This was, of course, great sport for Cassels and for the negro man who was driving; but I soon got even with them. I secured the mule to the cart, scrambled in again and we proceeded, the mule swimming in the deepest places. The water was so deep that it nearly filled the cart. We sat therefore on boards laid across the top, and those who wished to keep dry feet put them on similar boards placed in front. For my part I had no use for this last, for I was already wet. I therefore sat securely. The subaqueous roadway was a corduroy of huge logs, many of which had been carried away by the swift current, leaving deep holes. The jolting was something almost inconceivable. It was great sport and I enjoyed it hugely. I sat securely with my feet on the bottom of the waggon in the usual position and laughed until my sides ached while Cassels and the driver were bumped clean off the seats and fell on their backs in the water which nearly filled the cart.

Fairly landed on the other side, the mule and myself proceeded to the railroad. Now I preferred going along the track, for it was better walking and much shorter, but the mule had a different opinion, and neither persuasion nor force could induce him to take the track. After some delay and some vigorous argument to no effect, reason was compelled to yield to obstinacy and I took the waggon road although [it was] nearly twice as long. The familiar Jones' swamp I found deep, but not nearly so deep as [the] back swamp; the bottom, too, was smooth firm sand. I reached Johnson's station in the afternoon much too late to return to Doctortown the same day. I was therefore compelled to wait until the next day.

Jan. 19th.—Mine host at Johnson's station treated me with hospitality and even with unexpected kindness.

He seems really to sympathize with the refugees. I was very bountifully entertained and was quite surprised to find my bill this morning for supper, lodging and breakfast for myself and two days' entertainment for a negro man and horse only five dollars in Confederate money. Such a charge was only a cover for free hospitality. The old horse was so much rested that I determined to use him in the cart instead of the mule. I therefore mounted the mule, with the blanket for a saddle. When we got to Jones' swamp we took out two trunks, passed over without difficulty and returned for the other two. It commenced raining a little this morning soon after [our] passing Jones' swamp, the first sprinkle I have seen since I came to Doctortown.

When we reached [the] back-swamp ferry we found quite a scene of bustle and confusion—in fact we had heard a confused babel of noises long before we reached it. Cassels had several waggons and teams crowded with trunks, furniture and provisions of all kinds at the landing. Some of these goods were being carried over in the canoe, and some in a cart. The water is still rising, and is now almost impassable for horse and cart. The current is very swift and the bottom fearfully rough. The cart was driven by Cassels himself, standing in the floor, shouting, gesticulating and applying the whip. The reverberation of the shouting and hallooing of the driver and of the plunging and splashing of the horse amongst the great cypress trees and the great dark gloomy swamp filled with water could be heard a mile off. To stop would be fatal to success, so on he went, urging his horse to the utmost of his strength. He had previously attempted to cross with a waggon, but it had broken down and now stood dismantled in the road, rendering the middle passage still more hazardous.

I took the canoe, and as Henry knew nothing about the management of this, I must do the ferriage. From early boyhood I was skillful in the management of a canoe. The little dug-out was so narrow that it was unsafe to carry more than 300 pounds besides Henry and myself, and Henry must go along to lift out the trunks. The distance was half-a-mile and the current very swift. I took over the trunks one by one, making the passage each way five times.

Finally, Henry drove over the empty cart while I swam the mule over behind the canoe. The old horse did famously until within ten steps of the shore. Here on a very rough piece of the submerged corduroy road he stumbled and fell down, exhausted and utterly unable to rise. He would inevitably have been drowned had we not immediately jumped into the water up to the armpits and quickly released him from the cart. We then took hold of the wheels, brought the cart into shallower water, attached the mule and hauled it ashore in safety.

I now made arrangements with Cassels to join our forces until all our baggage was safe in Doctortown. He had four negro men, but I had a horse and cart. It was therefore a mutual benefit. Without this arrangement it would have been impossible to accomplish the transportation of my baggage, and I think the same might be said of Cassels. Since our first party passed over this ground not only has the back swamp risen greatly, and the swift current carried away and broken the flat on which the ladies crossed, but the rails have been taken up from all the trestles and embankments in order to repair the road higher up. The difficulties of transportation are therefore greatly increased. No pole-cars possible now. By the use of our two horses and carts, by nightfall [we] had transferred all the baggage, furniture and provisions to the railroad about three-quarters of a mile from the ferry landing and placed them safely under a rude shed by the roadside. Henry, faithful fellow, offered to remain here with the baggage during the night. Assured of their safety, I set off at a brisk walk to Doctortown, where I arrived at 8 P.M. Supper at the officers' quarters all over. Hungry and cold, I went into a cabin in which all the Liberty boys are quartered and therefore called "Liberty Hall." I found the boys just preparing supper. By cordial invitation I joined them with a right hearty good will, and then felt comfortable. Though still soaking wet to the skin, I then went to bed in Gen. McCay's quarters and slept soundly.

Jan. 20th.—Waked up this morning still very wet but feeling perfectly well. After breakfast I hired four negro men "camp boys" at five dollars a day to help me with the baggage, and without awaiting their slow lazy movements, went myself immediately to the scene of labour. Here under the shed previously mentioned I met Col. Hood, who had just come over the back swamp and had left Sister on the other side. It was raining hard, and Col. Hood was evidently very glad to see me and to resign his charge, and troubling himself no more went on to Doctortown.

I immediately set off and crossed the back swamp in the canoe, the rain falling in torrents. Anxious to save my shoes, my only pair, which are becoming ruined by constant walking and frequent wetting, I took off both shoes and socks and rolled up my pantaloons à la duck-hunter. In this costume I met and was introduced by Sister, with all formality, to Mrs. ———, who came out with her. The ladies were greatly shocked at my bare feet and legs. "Jump in, jump in," said I; "no time for ceremony now." I first took over in the canoe the two ladies; then returned for one of the drivers, who then went on to the shed with the ladies; then the trunks and bedding one by one; and finally Eliza, Sister's servant, and the remaining driver. The state of the water is such that we are compelled to leave the waggon and swim the mules over behind the canoe.

I had to make the trip nine or ten times before all was over, and had to do all the work myself, as neither of the men knew anything of the management of a canoe, especially in so swift a current. The cart and old horse again were used to transfer the baggage to the shed, where I left it in charge of the drivers, who were soldiers, and my man Henry, and took the ladies to Doctortown, where we arrived safely at 1 P.M.

Dinner over, I immediately returned to the scene of labour. On inquiry I found that the four negro men—lazy camp-loungers—whom I had hired this morning, when they felt the weight of the trunks shook their heads and went back to camp. Mr. Cassels' negroes and my man Henry, however, had worked faithfully. All Mr. Cassels' baggage and all the baggage brought out by me was already at the lake, but that brought out by Col. Hood was still at the shed. I set to work with all my might helping the negroes carry the baggage. The progress was very slow, for everything had to be carried a great portion of the way on the shoulders. At sunset a large portion was still at the shed.

I have worked very hard today, lifting heavy trunks in and out of the canoe, paddling the canoe at least ten miles in a swift current, and afterwards carrying trunks on my shoulders, together with a walk of about 8 miles. It has rained incessantly all day. I am still wet to the skin. In this condition I went to McCay's tent and went immediately to bed, Henry again remaining all night with the baggage, to take care of it.

The water has risen in the last 24 hours at least two feet. The back swamp is now entirely impassable for wheeled vehicles. Even one day's delay would have been fatal to my plans. Good judges say this is the greatest flood since the great Harrison freshet of 1841.

Jan. 21st.—With the dawn I was up and feeling perfectly well although still wet. By sunrise Cassels and myself were already across the lake and hard at work. During the forenoon we brought all of Sister's baggage to the lake, and much of Cassels' across the lake by boat, and to the Altamaha bridge by poling. In the afternoon we undertook to carry all the rest, namely, all of Sister's and much of Cassels', in one boat-load across the lake, intending thence to pole along the upper side of the embankment to the bridge.

This was the severest struggle we had to undergo. The great flood of water, while it facilitated the passage of the boat along the embankment, ran through the trestles with such fury that it was really dangerous to attempt the passage with our heavily laden boat. The negro men, three in number, were utterly useless as they had never used an oar in their lives. Cassels and myself therefore had to take the oars. These too were nothing but miserable makeshifts, made from inch planks. We got along, however, very well until nearly across the lake. Now the current became so swift that in spite of every effort to the contrary the boat was swept with violence against the trestle, and would have been carried through if I had not dropped my oar and laid hold of the pier. With the oars we now pushed against the piers with all our might and pushed the boat a little upstream. We now put out our whole strength rowing, to round, if possible, the point of the embankment, encouraging one another with shouts. Just as we were rounding the point, snap! goes an oar—"Quick, give me another!" Snap! goes another—"Quick, quick, another!" Another was grasped, but we had lost ground, and the struggle recommenced, but we were at least fifteen minutes making as many feet. We now poled the boat very leisurely along the upper side of the embankment until we reached the next trestle. There no human power could withstand the fury of the rushing torrent. We were carried with violence against the uprights and then whirled through and around with a velocity which in spite of our utmost efforts to the contrary carried us into the swampy woods on the lower side. Several gentlemen, experienced boatmen, who were standing on the embankment watching the struggles of our overloaded boat, declared afterwards that they expected every moment to see the boat either overturned or smashed.

What was to be done now? It was impossible to go along the embankment on the lower side, for this was full of drift-timber. We must go back through the trestle, or we cannot proceed. After a moment's thought I remembered that I had seen a canoe up the lake. I immediately got out on the embankment and ran over the trestle, back to the lake, secured the canoe and paddled back again as rapidly as possible. I pulled down about 100 feet of telegraph wire which I had seen hanging from the poles into the water, attached this to the bows of the boat and with the strength of five negro men on land a-hold of the wire and Cassels and myself assisting in the boat, sometimes by rowing, sometimes by laying hold of the piers of the trestle, after a half-hour's struggle we pulled through by main force against the pressure of the roaring torrent which rose almost to the gunwale.

At last [we] rounded the point and were safe on the upper side of the embankment in comparatively still water. From this point we poled along easily until the next and last trestle. There was secure walking on this one. We remembered our last experience. We therefore allowed the boat to drift along and towed it along by the wire, walking on the track, until we reached the embankment. From this point the negro men carried the baggage piece by piece on their shoulders to the bridge, where we deposited safely the last piece about 9 P.M.

I am completely exhausted tonight. Rain, rain again all day today. Again to bed with wet clothes. I have been wet to the skin every day and constantly for four days, but feel no inconvenience therefrom. I had scarcely laid down before I was fast asleep—"All with weary task foredone."

Jan. 22nd–23rd, Sunday and Monday.—Another Sunday, and another fresh start today. Made arrangements this morning to charter a box-car to carry all my luggage and Mr. Cassels' through to Thomasville. Brought all the baggage over the bridge in pole-car by twelve o'clock, and after drawing rations to last us to Thomasville, and without further incident worthy of record, arrived there on Monday evening, 23rd, 6 P.M. Mr. Samuel Varnedoe's carriage with his whole family were at the depot to receive Sister and carry her to their house, while I went again to kind old Mrs. Hayes—cheerful, cordial, good Mrs. Hayes.

Jan. 24th–25th.—Spent the next two days making arrangements to get on to Albany. After much difficulty I succeeded in hiring two waggons with mules and driver. The pay, 60 dollars a day and feed the mules. The trip will cost 400 dollars. Distance only 60 miles. It is true the money is Confederate but salaried officers like myself get but little even of that. Several ladies take advantage of the opportunity and join us. The party consists of Sister and her servant Eliza and her young child, two Misses Winn from Liberty with their servant-woman, Miss Crews from South Carolina. These with myself and the driver old Simon make eight without counting Eliza's baby. The baggage consists of thirteen trunks, besides rolls of bedding, carpet-bags, hat-boxes etc., a heavy load for two small waggons.

Jan. 26th.—Although I made every effort to get off early this morning the last words of the ladies detained us until 10 A.M. But Mrs. Young's, the stage breakfast-house, is only 15 miles; surely we can reach it before night. The roads, however, are in a dreadful condition, cut up by Government waggons and made worse more recently by the heavy rains. We stalled half-a-dozen times in the course of the afternoon, but our old wag-

goner Simon seems wonderfully expert in extricating
waggons from mud-holes. We make steady though slow
progress, Simon and myself walking all the way to relieve the load. About sunset we were within a mile and
a half of Mrs. Young's. We were all in high spirits in anticipation of a warm fire and a good supper, for the day
had been intensely cold and very rainy. Just then our
waggon made a fearful lurch, sank with one wheel deep
in the mud, and all our efforts at extrication failed. In
the meantime it was getting dark. It is impossible to ex-
tricate it without unloading. The ladies get down on
the wet ground, and get their thin shoes soaking wet.
We take everything out of the waggons before we can
get them out of the mud-hole. It had become now pitch-
dark. It is now impossible to proceed. We would stall at
every step. There is no alternative, we must camp out.
At this announcement the ladies looked very blank, but
there was no help for it. Simon and myself set about it
immediately, selected a dry spot, made a blazing fire,
hunted about in the dark until we found good water in
an old hurricane-root, then cooked and ate supper. The
ladies now looked more cheerful, but how shall they
sleep this bitter cold night? With the assistance of old
Simon I cut two poles, leaned them up at about an angle
of 30 degrees against two pines on the side towards the
wind, stretched a sheet over them so as to keep the wind
from the ladies' heads, [and] spread down a mattress and
plenty of bedding. On this the four ladies slept comfortably. For myself, I spread a rug before the fire, rolled
myself in a blanket, and slept soundly, waking up only
once to replenish the fire and get warm. Old Simon took
good care of himself, and of the two negro women.

Jan. 27th–28th–29th.—Bitter cold this morning. Water poured into the basin for face-washing freezes instantly. Cooked breakfast and got off early. Ladies suffered extremely in the open waggons today. I did not suffer at all, as I walked the whole day, partly to keep warm and partly to lead the mules. Roads are better today. Made about 20 miles and stopped at night at the house of Mrs. Adams, a very poor woman. She could give us shelter, but neither food nor bedding.

On the next day the weather was still extremely cold and windy, even colder than yesterday. The ground is hard-frozen even at midday. We get on very slowly, for we stop at every farm-house to get the ladies warmed. We are now in a very fertile and thickly settled country. Between Gumpond and Albany we meet many friends. At Gumpond I stop a moment at a very neat-looking cottage to make inquiries. As I knocked at the door a lady came forward whose commanding stature and magnificent queen-like beauty almost took away my breath. As I stood in speechless admiration and reverence, she recognized and greeted me heartily. It was one of the Misses Bacon of Liberty. To my great surprise and delight I found here not only Major Bacon's whole family except himself, but also old Mrs. Oliver Stevens, mother-in-law of my sister Ann. It was a very pleasant surprise on both sides. They overwhelmed me with questions about the people in Liberty, and urged me to stop, but we had no time. A few miles farther on, the ladies having become again extremely cold, I went up to another house to ask permission to stop and warm. As the gentleman of the house came to the door, I instantly recognized an old friend of our family whom I had not seen for twenty years—Granby Hillyer. I knew him as a young man, now he is hoary-headed. He greeted me very cordially and pressed us to stay at least a day or two with him, but of course this was impossible. After thawing our stiffened limbs, we therefore again went on.

About sunset we began to look out for a stopping place for the night. We were refused at several houses—"No provisions; no beds." We were beginning to be afraid we would have to camp out again—camp out in the midst of a thickly-settled country! But they have not felt the privations of the war here, or they would be more hospitable. I determined to make one more attempt. Yonder is a farm-house. I will try. Knock, knock! A servant came to the door. "Tell your master that ladies, refugees from the Coast, want lodging." Through the open door I heard the servant speak to her master, and her master say, "Tell the gentleman it is impossible, we are only camping ourselves." On the return of the servant to the door I did not even allow her to speak, but said immediately, "Tell your master I want to see him." When he came, to my astonishment I recognized Dr. Freeman, an old resident of Columbia, S. C. He immediately welcomed us and showed us every attention. In fact it seemed as if he could not do too much for us.

We so greatly enjoyed Dr. Freeman's open-handed hospitality that we slept late next morning (29th). It was Sunday—we were within seven miles of Albany—we could not get off from Albany at any rate till Monday morning—there is no use hurrying. So reasoned Dr. Freeman and his kind wife, and we felt the force of his reasoning. Nevertheless we got off between 10 and 11 A.M. and reached Albany about 2 P.M. We spent a very

pleasant evening with kind friends in Albany—R. K.
Hines and Mr. Hodge and others. The country from
Gumpond to Albany is extremely fertile, a rotten lime-
stone of the Eocene Tertiary Period. Along the road is a
succession of large plantations untouched by the war.
Jan. 30th–31st.—Started 8 A.M. to Macon by rail, and
arrived safely at 4 P.M. Found the rest of our party all
safe and waiting for us at the house of my niece Anna
Anderson. Spent the next day very pleasantly with our
many dear friends residing in Macon. The ladies want
rest—I want to make inquiries about means of transportation for my now large party and their baggage from
Milledgeville to Mayfield, where I hoped our difficulties
would be all over. We leave here the Misses Winn, but
take up my daughter Sallie and my niece Ada. Annie
will stay in Macon, for her husband Dr. Adams is stationed as surgeon here.

Feb. 1st.—"Omnibus at the door!" "Hurry, hurry—
no time to spare!" Alas, so much baggage, and so heavy.
All packed at last—"Goodbye, goodbye, goodbye all!"
And off we rattle at a sweeping trot, the driver plying
his whip at every step—"Quick, driver, quick; the whistle blows." Up to the depot we dash in a gallop as the
cars commence to move off. A young man in Confederate grey, seeing our situation, ran to the conductor,
stopped the train and kindly offered to assist the ladies
into the cars while I attended to the baggage. All ready!
Off we go! Young man still attentive. We joke Miss
Crews—her bright eyes and rosy cheeks must be the at-
traction, "Oh, dear no; it's Ada." The young man was
rather good-looking, bright, quick, efficient but withal
quiet and unobtrusive.

At Midway, one and a half miles from Milledgeville, we are left on the roadside. Beyond this the road is torn up by Sherman. Here we found a perfect babel of noise and confusion. Passengers in a great hurry and anxious to get on, waggoners taking advantage of their necessity to extort, our purse becoming very slender—can't afford such prices. The young soldier again comes to our relief, and quickly engaged two waggons for one-half the price which had been asked me. He is now regularly installed as one of our party. After a delay in Milledgeville which we employed in the society of many dear friends in that place, we started off again at 2 P.M. and without incident worthy of record stopped for the night at Mr. Kennedy's. We had food of our own supplied by kind friends in Macon and Milledgeville. We asked only shelter.

Mr. Davis (so he calls himself) is certainly a queer fellow. This companion whom we have picked up is quick, ready-witted, his senses all awake, observant, and yet *apparently* open and frank. Though so young,—only 20, he says,—he has evidently seen much of the world and pretends to be a great reader of character. There seems to be something mysterious about him. The young ladies don't know what to make of him. He attracts, yet repels. Sister thinks he is a Yankee spy. *He* says he is a Confederate spy—that he is a Kentuckian, a member of Lewis' Kentucky cavalry brigade—that he fought the Yankees all through Georgia with Wheeler. As we pass along from time to time he points out places of desperate conflict: yonder, under that tree, he killed a Yankee in self-defence; here he made a narrow escape, &c. Whatever he may be, he has taken a great liking to our party and is very kind and efficient. This night at Kennedy's, Mr. Davis and myself slept together. We lay awake and talked a long time before going to sleep. Our talk, commencing on indifferent matters, gradually became more and more serious, and he apparently opened his heart more and more. He is evidently a remarkable young man, intelligent, quick-witted and in the main worldly-minded yet not destitute of fine sentiments.

Feb. 2nd.—Mr. Davis' incessant bright conversation whiled away the tedium of today's drive to Mayfield. On the way, we passed through an encampment of soldiers. Mr. Davis tells us it is Stonewall's brigade of Hood's army—that they are on their way to Columbia to confront Sherman and assist in checking if possible his progress. He seems indeed to know everything in regard to both armies. Arrived at Mayfield 4 P.M. but too late to take the train for Augusta. The ladies concluded, instead of attempting to find a lodging-house, to take up quarters in the cars, which will leave tomorrow morning. I therefore went out and bought corn-meal and sweet potatoes, and with the assistance of Eliza, Sister's servant, I made a fire on the roadside, cooked our supper, and we all made a hearty meal, after which we settled ourselves in our seats for sleep.

Feb. 3rd.—Cooked and ate our breakfast of cornbread and sweet potatoes and started for Augusta at 9 A.M. Gen. Stovall,* who came into Mayfield last night, is on board the cars with us. He says that all Hood's army are on the way and will soon be in South Carolina to confront Sherman. His conversation cheered us very much as to our prospects. From the officers of his brigade I also heard much in defence of Hood's campaign in Ten-

* Brig. Gen. Marcellus A. Stovall.

nessee which I had always regarded as a great blunder. Arrived in Augusta about sunset. Here took leave of Mr. Davis. Said he as he shook hands, "I shall soon see you again in Columbia. The Yankees are certainly going there and I shall be wherever the Yankees are." Mr. Davis puzzles us more and more. He says his true name is *not* Davis, that he will sometime tell us what it is. He evidently knows all the officers of the army whom we meet and they know him. He knows all about our army, even to the minutest detail; and yet he is equally perfect in his knowledge of Sherman's army, the numbers of every corps and division, the officers &c., &c. He tells the most awful stories of his adventures, and yet he seems capable of doing all that he relates. The ladies seem to think that he can see right through bodies, corset, ribs—down into the very heart. They are fascinated, yet shrink from him—"Well, we will see him again in Columbia."

At Augusta our party separated and went to various private houses, Sallie and myself to Mr. T. P. Stovall's and the other ladies to Mr. William Adams' and Miss Crews to a friend in Augusta. Mr. Davis, I know not where.

Feb. 4th.—Sallie and myself started a little late this morning for the train for Columbia, which leaves before daylight. The rest of the party were to meet us at the depot. We must walk, for there is no vehicle to be gotten. The night was pitch-dark and raining. The streets in an awful condition from the recent freshets of the river which flooded the whole city. It is impossible to avoid puddles of mud and water, for we cannot see them. Dragging along poor frightened crying Sallie almost by force, "I skelpit on through dub and mire." There was not a moment to spare. We waded a good part of the way ankle-deep in mud and water. On reaching the depot we found all the rest of the party awaiting us. The depot was a scene of indescribable confusion. The whole of Stovall's brigade was going to Branchville to the scene of expected battle. The cars were all impressed for the purpose. We begged and entreated all sorts of officials. We insisted that our case was peculiar and very urgent. All to no purpose. Orders were positive. Besides, it is almost certain the road is already cut by Sherman's army and the cars cannot run through. Alas, Sherman is ahead of me again. But indeed why should he not be? There is nobody to oppose him. If he moves slowly it is only to pillage more thoroughly. The cars moved slowly off, and leave us on the platform shivering and disheartened. Slowly and sadly we turned away and by earnest invitation of Mr. Adams went all of us to his house.

After breakfast I went up to the Nitre and Mining Bureau office to see what could be done to help me. To my great delight I find there Prof. Holmes, Superintendent.* "Hello, Holmes, where from?" "Just from Edgefield." "When do you go back?" "Tomorrow." "Just the very thing." It was all arranged in a moment. Holmes will carry us to his house in Edgefield and thence send us in his carriage to Columbia, and Pratt, the chemist of the Bureau,† will send our baggage by Government waggon. I spent the rest of the day making arrangements for sending Miss Crews to her uncle's in Aiken. She is a bright, charming girl, and I shall miss her black eyes,

* Professor F. S. Holmes, superintendent of Nitre and Mining District No. 6, South Carolina.

† N. A. Pratt, bureau chemist.

her rosy cheeks and her naïve girlish manners. I got a passport for her from Gen. Fry,* the commandant of the Post. Gen. Fry confirmed what we had heard this morning at the depot. He said that it would be madness to attempt to go through by rail to Columbia, for the road was either already cut or commanded by the enemy near Branchville.

Feb. 5th, Sunday.—Again we start after a comfortable breakfast hour. Easy drive to Holmes' place in Edgefield. Holmes put us in the most cheerful mood on the way by his unquenchable spirits and kept us in roars of laughter with his inexhaustible store of anecdotes. Arrived at the plantation at 4 P.M. Holmes is a curious mixture of hospitable planter, ardent sportsman and devoted naturalist. The house is characteristic of the man—"every jutty frieze and coign of vantage" full of curiosities of natural history and trophies of hunting: the most astonishing buck horns, the most beautiful specimens of coral, fish skeletons exquisitely prepared, engravings of the great naturalists &c., &c. We were received with uproarious hospitality, quite characteristic of Prof. Holmes and his whole family. His own family is very large, some nine or ten, and quite a number of friends, refugees from the Coast, are now staying with him—and now our party of four and a servant. "No matter—the more the merrier—india-rubber house—room for plenty more." Then such a supper! It was a pleasure to sit down to the table, not so much on account of the abundance of good things as on account of the number of happy faces and warm hearts. About twenty sat down to the table together that night, and twenty happier people I never saw. After supper, sacred

* Brig. Gen. Birkett D. Fry.

music sung in chorus accompanied by the piano. And so we went to bed with our hearts still full of music—the music of kind feelings and happy hearts.

Feb. 6th.—Late breakfast—very late breakfast this morning. I was anxious to get off early, but no use to-day. Always late breakfast at Prof. Holmes' The family is so large it takes a long time to get up. The breakfast is so large it takes a long time to cook. Then after breakfast the plantation is so large that Prof. Holmes has many little things to look after. Then finally there are so many to take affectionate leave of, and the ladies have so many last words to say. Off at last, about 11 o'clock, young Holmes and myself in the buggy and the rest in the carriage.

Terribly raw and cold today, the wind blowing hard from the east and therefore directly in our faces. We stopped at a deserted church or school-house called Ridge Spring church, made a rousing fire, warmed our stiffened limbs, and cooked our dinner; after which we went on and stopped at Ridgel's for the night. Mr. Ridgel is an original character, a rough uneducated old man, shrewd, self-made and wealthy by his own exertions, querulous from constant bad health, vain of his wealth, of his shrewdness, of his second wife (now dead), who was evidently much above him in station, and of his daughter, who is rather good-looking, has had some schooling and plays tolerably well on the piano. He is a good type of rich overseer, and also of a "self-made man who worships his maker."

Feb. 7th.—Looked out upon a gloomy prospect this morning. Very cold, blowing, raining, sleeting, trees all covered with ice—and thirty miles yet to Columbia. But reach it we must, so we make an early start. After going about five miles the hind spring of the carriage broke. Our driver, however, is fertile in resources. Two elastic poles are quickly cut and properly adjusted and support the carriage very comfortably, so on we go. Suffered intensely from the cold today, sleet driving in our faces all the way. Stopped about noon for half an hour at the little town of Lexington. (Three weeks later I passed again along this road, but Lexington was not. A blackened ruin only remained in its place. Sherman had passed that way in the interval.) Here we warmed ourselves and ate our cold dinner. In the afternoon we easily drove to Columbia and reached that place about sunset. "Home at last!" Yes, home at last, *but* the indefatigable Sherman is again close by. I may be compelled to run again. Well, we will hope for the best. I will enjoy home while I can—"sufficient unto the day is the evil thereof."

Feb. 8th–15th.—This has been an anxious week for us all. The memory is burned into my brain. The enemy, swearing vengeance against South Carolina, the cradle of Secession, is approaching step by step, consternation and panic flight of women and children in front, and a blackened ruin behind. First we hear of them at Branchville, then at Orangeburg, then approaching Columbia by the Orangeburg road. Still the authorities—Beauregard, Hampton &c.—*seem* confident that they cannot take Columbia and that they will not attempt it. It is true the force here is a mere handful, some five to six thousand, but Hardee's corps is expected from Charleston, which, alas, must now be vacated by our forces, and Stuart's and Cheatham's divisions are expected from Augusta, and somebody else from some-where else—ah, expected! how often have we been cheated by "great expectations"!

During the week the Chatham Artillery arrive from the Coast, and we were made happy at least for a little while by the presence of my nephews John Harden and Julian LeConte. This artillery company will assist in the defence of Columbia; yes, assist, but this is not Hardee's army corps.

The enemy still approaches, and their guns are now distinctly audible. They are only a few miles on the other side of the river. John, Captain Green* and myself have put ourselves in daily communication with Beauregard and he has promised to give us the earliest information if it should become necessary to remove Government property of the Nitre Bureau now in our charge.

On the 10th I received orders from Richmond to remove the chemical laboratory to that place. I worked hard the 10th, 11th, 12th and 13th packing up. I got everything ready and sent them off to the depot early on the morning of the 14th. I was at the Charlotte depot all day trying in vain to get the boxes off. The depot is crowded, jammed to suffocation with people and freight both public and private trying to get off to Charlotte. On the morning of the 15th I again went to the depot and by much entreaty and considerable threatening I finally succeeded in getting the boxes on board and in charge of my assistant, Mr. Land, who will go with them. About 6 P.M. I again went down to the depot to see if they were actually off; they were indeed gone, and

* Maj. Allen J. Green, C.S.A., commanding post at Columbia.

my mind was relieved on that score. The depot is still crowded with people trying to get off. The panic is really frightful—women and children pleading to be taken aboard. It is difficult to see the surging, pleading mass and remain unmoved, it is difficult to resist the strong tide of human sympathy; still I try to remain calm. The authorities say there is no danger.

Capt. Green.

In a gloomy and anxious state of mind I turned homeward a little after dark. All day yesterday and today the booming of the enemy's guns seems to become nearer and nearer. Yesterday our first line of defence was carried. Today our second line was carried. How can the place stand? And the authorities talk confidently. Hardee is hourly expected, yes, surely Hardee will come in time. Such were my thoughts as I commenced to walk home. On the way I met an immense waggon-train half-a-mile long, rumbling slowly and softly through the unpaved streets on their way to the Charlotte depot. It was evidently an army train. Onward it slowly wound through the silent and deserted streets, hushed and still as if stealing away in the dark. Even the drivers urged their teams with bated voices. The solemn rumbling of this train as it dragged its slow length along smote painfully upon my heart. For the first time I utterly lost hope—"*Columbia is doomed!*"

On reaching home I found Mr. Davis there anxiously awaiting my return. Faithful to his promise made me in Augusta he had called on me yesterday and had then given me a rather gloomy account of the prospects of

Columbia, and advised me to leave as soon as possible. He now spoke in still more decided terms. He had come, he said, expressly to urge me to leave at once, not to wait until tomorrow, but to leave tonight. Tomorrow might be too late—the Yankees might be in Columbia by tomorrow. He had been in the Yankee camp all day—expected tonight to arrest a Yankee spy in Columbia, a woman and a citizen of this place. He professed to be intimately acquainted with the enemy's plans and to have much influence by bribery with many of the Yankee officers. On being asked what he thought of the safety of the city in case it fell into the hands of the enemy, he said he was actually afraid to tell us what he *knew* would take place, but he thought he could save *our* house and John's. "You must not be surprised," said he, "in case any Yankees should enter your house, to see me among them. If you recognize me don't betray me." He even offered to give letters to Yankee colonels if necessary. I declined, as I had no desire to have any connection with any tortuous policy.

Full of these sad tidings I went immediately over to John's and found him and Capt. Green consulting about going off at once. The military authorities had at last confessed that they could not hold Columbia, and had told Capt. Green that he had better leave as soon as possible and save what Nitre Bureau stores we could. Alas, alas! Hardee would not come, and no one knew where Stuart and Cheatham were.

We determined to leave at once, Capt. Green, John, his son Johnnie, about 15 years old, and myself. Together with the Nitre Bureau property, we determined by Davis' advice to take also all our valuables, as it was certain that the town would be sacked if not burned. On my own part I immediately set to work and packed up in trunks and boxes all clothes of the whole family, except what they had on and a change of underclothing, all the bedding except what was necessary to sleep on at home, all silver except one article apiece for the family, all jewelry, my manuscripts of unpublished works, notes of lectures &c., &c. These were all sent out at once to the Nitre and Mining Works on the northern outskirts of the town.

We all then took a sad heartbreaking leave of our families, left them to the tender mercy of God our common Father, and about 11 P.M. walked to the Nitre plantation. Here we remained all night making preparations to get off early in the morning. It was the saddest night I have ever spent in my whole life. The ominous words of Mr. Davis still rang in my ears: "I fear to tell you what scenes will be enacted in Columbia." The solemn booming of Sherman's guns gave fearful emphasis and meaning to those words. Our imperative duty required us to save what Government property was in our care. It was worse than useless for us to remain, as we would certainly be taken prisoners, all of us being officers, but it was hard to leave all that we loved most tenderly in the hands of the enemy—and such an enemy! "But I cannot believe, no I will not believe they will burn the city—yet they may; yes, they may! O God, protect our loved ones." I did not attempt to sleep. I sat by the fire all night with these thoughts throbbing in my brain.

Feb. 16th.—The booming of Sherman's cannon, which ceased about midnight, commenced again early this morning. We started soon after daybreak, about 6 A.M.

Our cavalcade consisted of two waggons, two carts and one buggy, all heavily laden. There were along four whites, already mentioned, and 22 negroes. Of these three were my own and three John's who begged to go with us. The rest were negroes hired on the Nitre plantation, men, women, children and babies. With the exception of the drivers these were all a sad encumbrance to us, but they were wives and children and relations of the drivers and desired and begged to go with us. We could not refuse them. Out of 100 negroes employed at the Nitre works these drivers had volunteered to go. Crawling so slowly along, everyone found it pleasanter to walk except the negro women with their children.

Our intention was to go to Allston and thence take the railroad to Abbeville. To take the Allston road it would be necessary to go back about a mile to town. It would have been much better, as it turned out, to have done so, but we were unwilling to lose at least two miles and, what was more important, an hour's time. The Winnsboro road passed close by the Nitre Works. We were informed that a little way on, a by-road crossed from the Winnsboro to the Allston road. It seemed much better to reach the Allston road through this by-road. Slowly we crawled along, for the roads were in an awful condition from much rain and long neglect. On reaching the by-road we were told that it was utterly impracticable for loaded waggons. We were advised to go on by the Winnsboro road ten miles to Killian's mill, and there we would find a good cross-road to the Allston road. We took this advice, as indeed we had now no alternative, and reached Killian's about 12 m. Here we stopped for lunch, to rest and feed the horses. We found indeed here the cross-road to which we had been directed, but as we followed it it became blinder and blinder, ramifying in all directions, and intersected by similar roads every few yards. We lost much time making enquiries and still more stalling on steep hillsides, until, about 4 P.M., we reached a swamp. In crossing this all the waggons and carts stalled and had to be unloaded to get them over. It was nearly dark before everything was safely across. It was clearly impossible to go any further. Here therefore we prepared to camp for the night. It was the most beautiful place for the purpose—a deep forest with spreading trees, oak and pine, pure water, plenty of oak leaves and pine-straw for bedding. To these attractions we soon added a blazing camp-fire. What more could we desire? Ah, how I could have enjoyed this camp in the woods but for my intense anxiety for loved ones at home. Our supper of cornbread and beefsteak was soon cooked and eaten. I then wrapped myself in my blankets with no shelter but the spreading trees and went to sleep with the booming of Sherman's artillery sounding in my ears and the last words of Davis still haunting my memory.

We have made only 15 miles today. Our camp in a direct line cannot be more than 10 miles from Columbia. The roar of artillery has been very distinct and incessant all day.

Feb. 17th.—We were waked up suddenly from deep sleep this morning about three o'clock by a fearful explosion which shook the ground like an earthquake even at this distance of ten miles. What can it mean? After remaining awake some time in great anxiety, I committed my dear ones to Divine protection and fell again into an uneasy slumber until daybreak, when we all got up and prepared to start as early as possible. After an early breakfast we harnessed up and were on our way by sunrise. The cannonading recommenced as usual this morning at daybreak, and soon became extremely rapid, in fact a continuous roar in which the separate explosions were scarcely distinguishable. We fear the explosion last night was the blowing up of our magazine, and this continuous roar of artillery is the covering of our retreat. (I afterwards learned that the explosion was the blowing up of the Charleston depot, containing large quantities of powder, by the careless use of lights of a band of negroes plundering—a large number of these were killed by the explosion.) Oh, what terror may our dear ones be suffering even now! About 9 A.M. the firing suddenly ceased entirely and was heard no more at all. This must mean the surrender of the city, or possibly the repulse of the enemy—let us hope for the best.

About 10 A.M. we reached the house of a Mr. Coon. I went up to the house to make enquiries about the road. As I approached, that old Coon eyed me as if I was a conscript officer. He seemed ready at any moment to take [to] a tree. I soon put him out of fear. He had, he said, left Columbia at 12 o'clock last night. He had lost his Company (the Senn's Home Guard),* and looked upon himself as a gone Coon if he remained in Columbia, so he came home as the safest place he knew of. He said, moreover, that everybody believed when he left that the city would be surrendered next day—that is, today. This is bad news indeed, but the man is a deserter and is evidently very badly scared. He may exaggerate.

* Post Guard, Post of Columbia, Capt. Rufus D. Senn.

Just before we came out into the Allston road we met several companies of Wheeler's cavalry, among whom were some friends from Liberty. They stated that they had been sent to Allston, but had been recalled to Columbia. What does this mean? Recalled to follow our evacuating army, or recalled to assist in defending Columbia? In answer, they said they knew nothing of what may have occurred in Columbia, but there were no Yankees about Allston. We were very much relieved to hear this. Our way seemed clear before us; there were no dangers ahead, at least.

On coming out into the Allston road we found it crowded with refugees from Columbia, some in carriages and buggies, some in waggons, most on foot, all panic-stricken, many way-worn, travel-stained but still hurrying on. Alas, how sad a sight! They all concurred in stating that Columbia was no doubt by this time in the hands of the enemy, although they had left before it was evacuated by our forces. We learned from these fugitives that we, after a full day and a half [of] travel, are now only 12 or 13 miles from Columbia. Here also we met Capt. Hughes of Liberty County, an old friend of mine. His face was badly burned. He informed me that he had left Columbia only about three hours ago— that the Congaree bridge was burned by our forces to cover our retreat—that he himself was defending the bridge, was the last man to leave it, and came very near being burned up with it—that Columbia was not actually surrendered when he left, but our troops were leaving as fast as possible and it was no doubt now in the hands of the enemy. He believes from what he heard from Wheeler's cavalry, just returned from Allston, that there was no enemy in that direction. Ah me, there is no resisting any longer the conviction that Columbia is indeed in the hands of Sherman.

We stopped for lunch near the 14-mile house. Here we met one of the Rhetts with an immense train of waggons, his man-servant and his maid-servant, his ox and his ass and everything that was his, including a drove of about 40 hogs and a flock of at least 50 turkeys, fleeing with all his family and substance from before the face of Sherman.

Today, though dry and clear and warm, the wind is blowing a perfect gale and the air is filled with smoke. What does this mean? Again the last words of Davis rang in my ears: "I fear to tell you what they will do." Oh, that I knew what would be, or perhaps is, the fate of Columbia! (This smoke, as we afterwards learned to our cost, was caused by the burning of the whole country about Allston by Davis' corps of Sherman's army. The strong north-west wind brought the smoke directly to us.) But no time now for indulgence of anxiety—we must hurry on. Past Rhett and his caravan making preparations for camp—(oh, that we also had stopped here!).

Crossed Little River bridge about 20 miles from Columbia about sunset. Soon after this we met a Lieut. Col. of Wheeler's cavalry, and learned from him that there was no enemy in the direction of Allston. "Good," said we; "there is no reason for anxiety on our own account. We at least are safe." Stopped about dark at a deserted house a little off the road. The house was full of peas, hay, fodder—abundant provision for our horses and a nice bed for man. "Ah, this now is pleasant." We cooked our cornbread, roasted our potatoes, ate heartily and conversed rather cheerfully until 10 P.M.—Pleasant, yes, very pleasant were it not for Mr. Davis' last words still ringing in my ears. Nevertheless, at about ten o'clock I threw myself amongst the peas and with an ejaculated prayer for the loved ones at home I soon fell asleep. Alas, alas! while we thus slept in peace Columbia was wrapped in flames! If we had even looked at the sky in that direction before going to bed and seen its ruddy glare, we would have slept none that night.

Feb. 18th.—I had had a good night's rest, had eaten a hearty breakfast. The morning was clear and bracing, but not cold. My physical system was in fine condition and strongly disposed me to take a favorable view of the situation. It was not absolutely certain that Columbia had fallen—let us hope it has not. Or supposing it has fallen, I cannot believe that Sherman will deliberately burn it. We have been assured in the most positive manner by officers and men of Wheeler's command that there is no enemy in front of us. What shall prevent us then from being cheerful? We *were* cheerful. The glorious morning and perfect digestion drove Mr. Davis' ominous words out of my mind. The roads, it is true, were still in awful condition so that we stall every few hundred yards, but we continue to creep on at the rate of about two miles an hour—"but no use in hurrying, no enemy ahead." As usual, John and Capt. Green are a little ahead in the buggy. This glorious bright morning I prefer walking. Johnny sometimes joins me and sometimes is perched high on the trunks and bedding-rolls in the waggons. Johnny has been sick and is not strong. The negro women and children are all in the waggons. I was walking along rapidly and with a springing step a little ahead of the waggons. I was just passing a country cabin about a hundred yards from the road. Suddenly I heard, "Stop, Mister; stop!"

I stopped, looked around and saw a country woman rapidly approaching from the house. "Where are you going?" "To Allston," said I. "To Allston! Don't you know the Yankees are crossing Broad river not more than a mile from here? My father is expecting them at our house every minute." "Impossible!" said I. "We met Wheeler's men not more than a mile back, and they assured us there were no Yankees ahead. They ought to know, for they were sent here to watch them." "Wheeler's men!" retorted she contemptuously. "Don't you see that smoke yonder? And that one there? and that one yonder? and yonder—and again yonder?" pointing rapidly in different directions. I looked, and to my utter dismay I saw the columns of the smoke of burning houses on every side, some in front, some on the right and some on the left. Some were behind and not more than half-a-mile distant. We were in the midst of the enemy whom we thought so far away. They had just commenced their morning's work of destruction. Soon the popping of guns with which I had become so familiar in Liberty commenced, and continued incessantly.

While I was talking to the woman, John and Capt. Green had gotten about a quarter of a mile ahead and right towards the enemy. I ran towards them at my best speed, whooping and hallooing at the top of my voice until they stopped. A few words, and the rising columns of smoke on every side, quickly explained the situation. We consulted together a moment—what was to be done? It was clearly impossible to turn back, for the Yankees are all around, behind as well as before. Our mules even with lashing and whooping cannot be made to make more than two miles an hour.

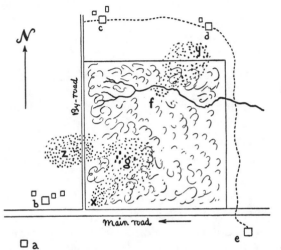

Patch of forest where we attempted to save our waggons.
(Marks of reference are explained in text.)

We determined to turn into the woods and remain hidden until the Yankees had passed on—perhaps it will be but for a few hours. The chances of escape seemed small, very small, it is true, but to go on or turn back was certain ruin. There happened fortunately to be just where we stopped a thick forest about half-a-mile square on one side of the road. We took down the fence, drove the waggons into the woods, put up the fence again (of course this was of the rail variety), carefully erased the waggon tracks, then drove the waggons deep into the forest and into the centre of a thick clump of saplings (at g), and after unharnessing carried the mules, the provisions and the negroes about 100 yards farther on into a deep hollow through which ran a stream, and made camp (at f).

This being accomplished to our satisfaction, leaving John and Johnny with the waggons, Capt. Green and myself went out to observe the enemy in order to ascertain if possible when they would leave the vicinity and where they would go. Coming to the main road, therefore, but keeping ourselves concealed in a thick clump of pine saplings at the place marked x, we were not long in discerning seven Yankees approaching a house about 300 yards distant. This house is marked a in the sketch. They did not burn the house, but remained there half an hour. Just then 7 or 8 of Wheeler's men rode up to where we were standing and accosted us. The Yankees saw them. Each party was evidently afraid to attack the other—the Yankees moved off rapidly in one direction, while the Confederates rode off equally rapidly in the other.

From our hiding place (x) we saw several parties of Yanks approach the same house during the day. Meanwhile the popping of Yankee guns, the squealing of Confederate pigs and the cackling of rebel chickens were incessant all around us. About 11 A.M. a dense column of smoke, then the squealing of pigs and the cackling of hens, then the sound of human voices in loud and angry altercation proclaimed in unmistakable language that the house nearest us and only 100 yards from where we were standing was fired. (This house, marked b in the sketch, I afterwards learned was the house of a Mr. Mc-Connell, an old man of some influence in the neighbor hood, and a staunch Confederate.) Presently another and still another column of smoke shot up, as one and then another out-building was fired and consumed amid the shouts of infuriated demons. In a few minutes, their work being done, the measured tramp of armed men was heard approaching, and several companies passed along the main road to the south of us and along the by-road to the west. They passed within 20 yards of us as we lay concealed and watching them, and within 150 yards of our waggons. In about a half-hour columns of smoke to the north and north-east announced that two more houses (marked c and d) had been fired. As other companies continued to pass along the two roads mentioned, our position so near the roads was too dangerous. I therefore went down to the camp, told John what I had seen, and then crossed the stream, secreted myself in a thick clump of saplings to the north-east [and] crept on my hands and knees close to the burning house (d). From my position (marked y) I could distinctly see all that took place. In a few minutes the hum of many approaching voices caused me to lie very close. Two companies of Yanks leading a half-dozen horses and mules taken from the burning stables passed within twenty or thirty steps of me and went on towards the main road. (The dotted line shows their course.) I followed them. They went to a house (marked e) on the south side of the main road, the same I believe from which the woman came who halted me this morning. They did not burn, but the popping of guns, the squealing of pigs and cackling of hens proclaimed the object of their visit. I returned to camp and reported what I had seen. It was now 2 P.M. I had been following and watching the Yanks all the morning. We were too anxious to care for dinner, but the negro children and especially the babies were not disturbed in mind. They were hungry—we had nothing cooked and dared not make a fire; they were only kept quiet by the threats of the older negroes. We hope the Yanks are going farther, for although we see from time to time new columns of smoke, these seem to be at some distance. I prowled about the whole afternoon, but saw no Yankees. We were beginning to hope that they had all passed on. We were soon undeceived, however, for towards sunset they began to return to camp. They had only been foraging—their camp had not moved.

Soon after dark we saw their camp-fires on Broad river about a mile off, heard the rolling of their drums, and the cheering as party after party returned to camp with their booty.

In the meantime the negro children were becoming clamorous for food—they had had nothing since morning. It was absolutely necessary to make a fire and cook. With many misgivings and many directions to make it as small as possible, we consented. Alas, alas! these crying children, the low whimpering of the hungry mules as fodder was brought to them, and, more than all, that fire, that dreadful fire, will surely betray us. The negro men concealed the fire as much as possible by constructing a thick screen of boughs, but still the reflection on the tree-tops above is fearfully distinct. As soon as possible the fire was extinguished, and we went to bed. Anxiety of mind kept us from sleep until late. Our fate will probably be decided tomorrow.

Gradually the hum of the Yankee camp ceased and all was still as death. I lay awake a long time gazing as I lay into the tranquil heavens studded with innumerable stars, and the huge oaks standing like giants with arms uplifted and faces upturned to the sky. Slowly the deep tranquillity and holy calm of nature transfused itself into my soul, and I sank quietly to sleep.

Feb. 19th, Sunday.—We got up this morning in fine spirits: we have not been discovered yet (so we thought); the fine bracing morning exhilarated us in spite of our danger. We cooked and ate our breakfast before sunrise, so that the fire might be extinguished before the Yankees were stirring. It was now a little before sunrise. For greater security Capt. Green is out acting as picket while the rest of us ate. I had just finished a very hearty breakfast, was just then wiping my mustaches and enjoying the irrepressible sense of comfort indissolubly connected with perfect digestion, when the measured tramp, tramp, tramp of marching toops was distinctly heard and presently the many forms of men were seen through the trees, passing along the by-road. There seems to be a full regiment. They passed within 100 or 150 yards of us. We drew a long breath when they were fairly gone. They had not observed us. The digestive process interrupted by this alarm had just recommenced when a sharp cry of "Look out!" broke the stillness of the early morning air. "Dat's Cap'n Green say, 'Look out,'" said Sandy, my negro man. Fearing something wrong I started immediately for the waggons, where I had carelessly left my pistol, and my carpet-bag containing many R.R. bonds, notes of lectures, Mss., also silver, jewelry etc., on rising from bed to go to breakfast. When I reached the lower waggon I saw the Yankees already swarming upon and pillaging the uppermost. I had no time to secure anything. I was within ten steps of them before I saw them. I instantly dropped to the ground where I stood and then stealthily but swiftly ran in a crouching position into a thicket of pine saplings (g) and there watched their operations from a distance of about thirty yards. Some of them commenced immediately knocking to pieces trunks and boxes, rifling their contents. Others scattered in all directions, apparently searching for concealed treasure or hiding Confederates. I quickly saw that it was impossible to remain where I was. I therefore changed my position to a little greater distance, and again and again changed as they approach with widening range, until finally I crossed the by-road and concealed myself at the place marked z. I could not *see* any longer but could distinctly *hear* the work of destruction going on vigorously for an hour or more. After this all became quiet again. I was now extremely anxious to go down to the waggons to learn the extent of the damage, to save if possible my papers and Mss. (money I took for granted gone), and more than all to learn the fate of the rest of the party. This, however, was now impossible, for the enemy in large numbers were constantly passing along the by-road within five steps of my hiding place. Repeatedly during the morning I was in imminent danger. Once a tall Yankee—he seemed to me *enormously* tall—left the road, came straight towards me as I lay concealed, stopped within six feet of me, laid down his gun, took off his canteen and haversack, arranged something about his person, slung on his canteen and haversack, took up his gun and went on.

Finding the clump of saplings in which I was hidden so small and so near the road along which the Yankees were constantly passing, I determined if possible to re-cross the road and get nearer the camp. Between 8 A.M. and 12 M. I repeatedly made the attempt, but every time was very near being discovered by passing soldiers. About noon I finally succeeded. I now crept cautiously down on my hands and knees towards the waggons. How often have I practised this mode of progression in duck and turkey hunting—now I am the quarry! As I approached I heard the negroes talking. I will go up, I thought, and at least learn the fate of John and his son. When within about thirty yards, I heard the voices and saw the forms of Yankees as well as negroes—the latter were apparently expostulating. It was evidently a second party. I crept a few steps nearer and watched them. They piled the boxes and trunks on the waggons and set fire to everything. Four columns of smoke—four forked and leaping flames—a little crackling and roaring for fifteen minutes or so—perhaps a half-an-hour, and then all was quiet again and only a little ashes left. This done, the Yankees began again to scatter and search the woods, and again I had to fly.

I next selected a hiding place to the north-east of the camp near the place (marked *y*) where I had hidden yesterday. I justly reasoned that the house near by, having been burned, would not be visited again. Here therefore I was comparatively safe, but my extreme anxiety concerning the fate of my brother and nephew rendered it impossible for me to remain quiet. Three or four times in the course of the afternoon I crept down on the camp, but in every case I found straggling Yankees there and had to retreat. My anxiety increased every moment—may I never again pass such a day of agony!

It was now growing dark—the camp-fire, I see, is burning. I determined at any risk to make another attempt. I again creep down on my hands and knees, closely observing at every step, until I come within ten steps of the camp-fire. I see there is no one at the fire but one little negro boy about eight years old. The little fellow started up to run—"Stop!" said I. He at once recognized me and obeyed. "Where are Sandy and Charles?" "Dey all up wey de waggon been." "Go tell them I am here." While he was gone I thought to myself, "There may be Yankees with them. I will step a little ways into the bushes and observe them as they come."

In a little while all the negroes came down to the fire, and seeing no Yankees among them I immediately came forward. "Oh, Mossa! I so glad to see you safe!" They exclaim it with one voice. "Where's John?" I asked. "Oh, my Mossa, my dear Mossa, dem Yankees take Mass John and Mass Johnny right off wid dem." "Great God! Why didn't he run?" "I dunno, my Mossa. I dunno. Mass John could-a got away easy; but he walk right up to de Yankee, and de Yankee put he gun right to he breas' and he gie hisself right up." "Was it because he did not know what to do with his son?" (Johnny had had the measles and was still feeble.) "I speck so—yes—I t'ink so maybe." "And where is Capt. Green?" "Dunno, but t'ink Cap'n Green mus' be in de woods some way." "Have you got anything to eat? I am almost famished!" "I put 'way dis berry piece of meat and bread for you," said Charles, as he handed me a piece of boiled pork and a piece of rough cornbread. I felt ravenous, but can't eat but a few mouthfuls.

I now noticed for the first time that I did not see my

two negro boys, Billy and Alfred, among the assembled
negroes. "Why, where's Billy and Alfred?" I asked.
"Dem Yankee take off Billy and Alfred and Mass John
t'ree boys wid dem to ride de mule."—"Dey beg to stay,
but dey make dem go." "Poor negroes!" I thought, "what
will become of them!" Sandy and Charles then told me
that they wished to take the negro men also, but that
they had begged to be allowed to stay to take care of
the women and children in their charge.

I then asked after my property, especially my notes
of lectures and my manuscripts. "All gone—ebry bit
gone," they said. The silver, jewelry and men's clothing
they took with them, the rest were burned with the waggons. The first party contented themselves with the most
valuable things; the second party took much that was
left and burned the rest. Since then, party after party
had been there searching for concealed treasure and
hiding Confederates. They knew that two of us had
escaped, and even mentioned our names. They swore
that they would beat every bush, but they would find
us next day. This they might easily do, for (as seen by
the sketch) the wood was only about $\frac{1}{4}$–$\frac{1}{2}$ mile square
and surrounded on every side by open cultivated fields.

I had now warmed myself and gotten all the information I could. I deemed it unsafe to stand any longer in
the bright light of the camp-fire. I therefore told Charles
and Sandy that I would go a little way into the woods,
indicating the place, and that if Capt. Green came in,
one of them must come and tell me. I had not been absent from the fire more than ten or fifteen minutes when
Charles came to inform me that Capt. Green had come
in and wished to speak with me. I came immediately to

the fire, but saw no Capt. Green. "Where is he?" I asked. "In de woods up dey," said Charles, pointing in the direction of the burnt waggons. I went in the direction indicated, but still no Capt. Green. I walked about in the pitch darkness for some time without finding anyone. I began to suspect a trick to capture me. I remained perfectly still and listened intently, but all was silent as death. I whistled a long low whistle—no answer. I whistle again a little louder—after a while a very low, cautious whistle in reply and very near me—what does it mean? I walked in the direction of the whistle, then stopped and listened. Presently I heard the crushing of dry leaves under cautiously approaching footsteps. Soon it stopped. "Captain!" said I in a loud whisper. No answer. "Captain!" I called a little louder. Still no answer—what can he mean? I approached still a very little nearer and stood behind a huge oak. "Hist, Captain!" said I, still louder. "Doctor, is that you?" I heard in [a] hoarse whisper. "Certainly it is I, why are you so hard to find?" I asked as I now came forward and extended my hand, which he eagerly grasped. Poor Captain! He was very much exhausted from *want of rest* (he had scarcely slept at all the previous night), *want of food* (he had eaten nothing since supper last night, for he was scout while we ate breakfast), *cold* and *constant anxiety*. We then went to the fire, and while the Captain warmed himself, for greater security we placed several negroes in various directions as pickets.

While the Captain thus stood absorbing the genial warmth of the camp-fire I related what I had learned from the negroes, and the adventures through which I had passed. In turn he then related his own experiences.

It seems he had been concealed *all day* on the other side of the by-road in the same clump of saplings which I had used for the same purpose from 8 A.M. until 12 M. We were therefore very near each other without knowing it. He had been lying flat among the dead branches of a fallen pine all day—in the most exposed position possible, for it was near the angle between the two roads, along both of which Yankees were continually passing (not far from the point marked z). The danger had seemed to him so great that he had not dared to change his position since 6 o'clock this morning. Once several Yankees sat on the trunk of the fallen tree in the branches of which he lay concealed and within 3 or 4 yards of him, and conversed there for some time. He learned from the conversation of these Yankees that a

"Hist, Captain!"

certain "nigger named Jim" had discovered us the previous night by our fire and the crying babies, and had revealed his discovery to the Yanks early this morning. No wonder the Captain is exhausted, for what I had suffered in that clump for four hours he had endured all day. Yet I think he might have extricated himself, as I did.

We had been conversing for about 15 minutes when one of our pickets came running in, saying, "Somebody comin'." We were off into the woods in a trice. After a few minutes we received signal to come forward. We did so, and found just arrived my boy Billy, John's boy London (John's two other boys, Peter and Somerset, were never heard of after). With these was a boy hired at the Nitre plantation, and my other boy Alfred came in soon after. They had escaped from the Yankees, they said, and had come back from Allston. On inquiry, they told me that the Yankees had carried John and Johnny as far as Allston—six miles—, that John's watch had been taken from him but had been restored at Allston by order of the captain to whom he had reported the robbery, that they had not been harshly treated, but had been compelled to walk all the way. While we were talking, another picket came running in, saying, "Somebody comin'." In an instant we were again concealed; again a false alarm—[it was] only [that] one of the negro men had been up to the burnt waggons and was returning.

My man Sandy now took me aside and told me privately that the Yankees had not burned up absolutely all the ladies' clothing, but had given quite a considerable quantity to the negro women, who had them concealed, and that it was this fact which gave so much interest to the place where the waggons had been burned—that they were about that business when I first came to the fire this evening. I took Charles, who is the leader of the whole company of Nitre Bureau negroes, and questioned him on the subject. He admitted that such was the fact, but added in extenuation that if the women had not begged for them they would have been burned. He promised, however, to save what he could and carry them back to Columbia. I told him I would pay him well for everything he brought back.

We must not stay in these woods another day. It was hardly more than a quarter of a mile square. The Yanks had sworn they would find us the next day, if they had to beat every bush. I therefore called Sandy and Charles to me. I paid Sandy twenty dollars to carry my negro boys and John's London and Robert back home, and Charles a hundred dollars to carry back the negroes belonging to the Nitre Bureau. I could no longer take care of them—they must shift for themselves, and so would I. They would find no difficulty in returning, for they were the "privileged class." I must lie in the woods some time yet. I then shook them each heartily by the hand, sent messages by Sandy to our families, tied up my meat and cornbread in my handkerchief and again bade them goodbye. "Goodbye, Mossa, and God bless you"—"Take care of yourself, my dear Mossa"—"I hope de Lawd will keep you f'um dem Yankee." Such were the parting words which saluted me on every side as we moved off. Were they sincere? I thought so then. I think so now. I was really deeply moved by their kindness—and yet, and yet I now know that they were anxious for us to leave not only for our own safety, but also and perhaps chiefly because they had some of our property which they did not desire or expect to return. Were all their expressions of kindness, then, pure hypocrisy? No; there was I am sure real sincerity and kindness. Of such mixed stuff is woven our human nature, especially negro nature.

We left the camp-fire about 9 P.M. We had nothing in the world in the way of clothing except what we had on our backs. Fortunately, when the waggons were captured I had on my overcoat and Captain Green a blanket arranged with a draw-string so as to be worn as a cloak and hood. I took my direction by the stars, struck through the woods and quickly reached the main road. We walked on rapidly but silently in the direction of Columbia. Captain Green's tall, gaunt figure with his short blanket-cloak with its cowl-like hood and his long limbs moving below presented a very solemn appearance. We had heard from the negroes (who got it from the Yankees) that the Little River bridge was burned, and we supposed by the Yankees. If so, then evidently they did not expect to go in that direction. If we could get across the river, we reasoned, we would be comparatively safe. Our plan therefore was to cross the river to-night and then tomorrow to move slowly and cautiously towards Columbia, whence the Yankees had all gone.

On we went therefore, rapidly but in silence, I in front, Captain Green behind. As we pass along we notice burning houses on either side. The deserted house in which we lodged two nights ago is now smouldering ashes. We are now within half-a-mile of Little River bridge. The death-like stillness was broken only by our own echoing footsteps on the hard, frozen ground, which seemed painfully loud and distinct.

Suddenly we heard the sound of light footsteps close behind us. Turning quickly around we saw a tall, well-dressed, intelligent-looking negro man almost treading on our heels. He must have crept up on us. "Hello,

Captain Green's blanket-cloak as worn three ways.

where are you going?" said I. "I am going home," said he. "Where is your home?" "Just up dere on de hill." Looking in the direction in which he pointed, we saw a house, brilliantly lighted up by a blazing fire on the hearth, not more than two hundred yards from the road. "Who lives there?" we asked. "Nobody but some colored folks." "Yankees trouble you much?" "Lawd! yes suh, very bad all day. I afraid dey will come back tonight." "Who burned Little River bridge, Yankees?" "No suh, Wheeler's cavalry." "How do you get across?" "Dere's a big log layin' across 'bout 300 yards above de bridge." "Good night." "Good night, suh." He turned up through a gateway, and went towards the house while we went on. In that house at that very time were quartered a number of Yankees. We deeply suspected that the negro would inform on us, but had no idea the Yankees were so close at hand.

We had left the house about a quarter of a mile [behind us] and were about the same distance from the burned bridge. From the point where we now were commences an embankment which, becoming higher and higher [as it goes] to the river, forms there an abutment for the bridge. We were just about to

Mysteriously followed.

enter on this embankment—"*What's that?*" said Captain Green, suddenly stopping. The clatter of horses' feet galloping from the house of the "cullud folks" towards the main road was distinctly heard. We stopped and listened intently—will they come this way or turn the other way? They turned *towards* us. They are not more than two hundred yards distant. The road here runs through a ploughed field. There is absolutely nothing to conceal us but the rail fence on either side. There is not a moment to spare. In an instant we were over the fence and closely squatted each in his own fence-corner. We had hardly gotten settled when the Yankee cavalry came dashing by. To avoid the mud, the horses turned close to the fence on *our* side. The horses' hooves struck the very rails against which we were lying. As they passed one by one I counted them. There were just twenty. As soon as they were gone I went over to Captain Green's fence-corner and consulted with him as to what we should do.

We had scarcely commenced to speak together when we heard them coming back. They had apparently examined the long embankment to the river, and satisfied themselves that we were not there. Crouching again each in his own fence-corner we listened to their approaching steps with beating hearts. On they came, but instead of passing again as we had hoped, they reined up suddenly just where we were and commenced dismounting. Now, thought I, we are gone, for they are going to search the fence. As the road was muddy the whole party, some on horseback and some dismounted, stood close to the fence, the dismounted ones leaning up against the fence itself. I could easily have put my hands through the rails and taken hold of one fellow by his breeches legs. But *I didn't.* I didn't move a muscle, and scarcely breathed. And there they stood chatting pleasantly for half-an-hour. Of course I overheard every word. They spoke first of fugitive Confederates and bushwhackers. In this connection Captain Green says he overheard them mention our names. They spoke then of Cheatham's corps, its position and probable strength, &c.

At last one of them who seemed to command the squad said, "Let's try this way." They quickly mounted and away they galloped in the direction from which we had come. I can only account for this by supposing they had concluded that we, suspecting the negro, had turned back on our tracks as soon as he was out of sight—the very thing we would have done had we known the Yankees were in the house at that time. I learned afterwards from Sandy that these same horsemen came to our camp looking for us about twelve o'clock that night; that is, soon after they left us.

I listened to their retreating footsteps until they became faint, then rose, drew a deep breath and went to see how Captain Green fared. Can that small, dark-grey bundle be Captain Green, or is it a gigantic toad? If it be indeed the Captain, what has become of his long legs? I poked him with a stick—"Captain, is this you?" The grey bundle slowly stirred, lifted itself up, expanded itself to the altitude of six good English feet— my stick was a magic wand, nay more, it was the spear of Ithuriel, for it had suddenly transformed that shapeless mass into Captain Green in his true lineaments and his majestic proportions—a little shaky about the knees, a little tremulous in voice, a little unsteady on his pegs, but otherwise quite natural.

We listened intently yet for a little while. The trampling grew fainter and fainter and finally ceased. Still we listened in silence. "Doctor, is not that talking I hear in the road a little ahead of us?" I listened and thought I too heard talking. "Yes, I think so," said I. We accordingly struck into the field in a direction at right angles to the road until we were completely concealed by the darkness, then down to the river, then by the river-bank until we came to the burning bridge. "Doctor, has it not become very cold?" "It does indeed seem so." We had been very comfortable a half-hour ago, and now our teeth are chattering. "It must be the frost hanging about the river." "Perhaps so," said I. After a little while the weather seemed to moderate again. "Maybe it is the Yankees and not the river," suggested I. "Maybe so."

Captain Green and myself hiding from the Yankee cavalry.

It was now midnight and very dark. The banks of the river are steep and very muddy. It is impossible to cross the river without more light. The moon does not rise until four A.M. We must wait. We sat on a log in a dry place at the foot of a huge white oak which spread its great long bare arms in every direction over a huge area. I had eaten but little before leaving the camp. My appetite now returned. The abutments of the bridge were still burning. I climbed up the steep embankment, broiled my bacon and toasted my cornbread and ate heartily. After thoroughly warming myself I returned, as it was much too conspicuous standing in the light of the fire. On returning I tried to persuade Captain Green to take food, but he had no appetite. The night was growing very cold, the Captain was suffering very much from cold and exhaustion. "Go and warm yourself by the fire, Captain." "No, I cannot climb the embankment; besides, it is too conspicuous." For hours I paced back and forth, walking rapidly, stamping my feet, swinging my arms, striking my chest to keep warm. Meanwhile the captain sat on the log in a state of complete exhaustion, his head sinking lower and lower on his knees. . . . "Let him sleep!"

While the Captain sleeps, let us explain the situation. Little river, like all rivers which periodically overflow their banks, is flanked on either side by natural levees; that is, by banks considerable higher than the low grounds a little farther back. We had chosen this natural levee as the dryest place we could find. In order to drain the fields bordering the river a ditch had been cut through the levee to the river. Where it cuts through the highest point of the levee it was about six feet deep and only one foot wide. Captain Green was sitting on a log close by the ditch. As I passed back and forth I observed him nodding from time to time and his head sinking lower and lower on his knees. Presently I heard behind me an agonizing cry of "Oh! Oh! Oh-h!" I turned about quickly, but Captain Green had disappeared as if the earth had swallowed him up. I ran to the spot and found to my joy that his great top boots were still visible. I was just about to lay hold of these to haul him out when they disappeared suddenly and his cowled head appeared in their place, with face all begrimed with mud. In spite of the seriousness [of our situation] I could not for laughter help him for some time. Finally I got him resurrected and placed like a tub on its bottom again, "Why, what on earth were you doing down there, Captain?" said I, as soon as I could control myself. "I can't tell," said he. "I suppose I went to sleep and nodded headlong into the ditch. When I woke up I found myself standing on my head." "Are you hurt?" "Not much except this bruise." There sure enough was a severe bruise on the side of his forehead where he struck the bottom of the ditch. After a little the Captain, afraid to trust himself in a sitting posture, got up and commenced searching for a good crossing place. He went staggering about in an uncertain manner, like one drunk with sleepiness and exhaustion. Passing near the ditch

Captain Green, asleep, falls into a ditch, and I am disconsolate; but he comes to, and I pull him out. A progressive picture.

again, but not perceiving it, he again suddenly disappeared in its depths. Hauled out again, he declared that he had again fallen asleep while walking, and was entirely unconscious until awakened by the shock at the bottom of the ditch. The proper treatment in such cases is given by Butler in his "Hudibras":

> He gently raised the Knight
> And set him on his bum upright.
> To rouse him from lethargic dump
> He tweaked his nose with gentle thump,
> Knocked on his breast as if 't had been
> To raise the spirits lodged within.

In the confusion of the moment I did not remember this admirable recipe, and I am afraid I lacked something of the affectionate manner of Ralpho. However, I did what I could and succeeded in restoring him. The fact is, the poor Captain, naturally feeble at best, is so prostrated by want of food and rest, by constant excitement of mind and exposure to cold, that he can scarcely stand.

At last the moon rose, not in clouded majesty apparent Queen, but a thin meagre crescent obscured by mist, stealing into the heavens as if ashamed of herself. The light was scarcely improved at all by her presence. We, however, went up the river three hundred—four hundred yards, but could not find the cross-log. We came back to the bridge and examined the river more carefully. We found it there a foaming rapid which was evidently shallow and with rocky bottom. With some difficulty we got down to the river, and then easily waded across—it was not more than knee-deep.

Feb. 20th.—We crossed Little river about five A.M., an hour before daybreak. The cold and mental excitement, which only braced my muscles, completely paralyzed the Captain. The effort of crossing the river was too much for him. There was a steep ascent from the river, where we crossed, up to the road. I commenced ascending this at a rapid rate, when I heard behind me, "Oh, Doctor, Doctor!" Looking back I saw Captain Green sitting on a stump, completely broken down. I immediately went to him. He was breathing heavily, with a very severe pain through his chest (he has but one perfectly sound lung). "Doctor, I can't go any farther, you must leave me." "No, Captain, I won't leave you. Take my arm—I will help you up the hill." After recovering his breath he did so, but even with this help he had to stop every ten steps and sit down to rest. After reaching the main road he got along a little better, but even here on level ground he could not walk more than two or three hundred yards without stopping to rest. I had intended to go four or five miles beyond Little river on the road towards Columbia, then take to the woods and be governed by circumstances. I afterwards learned that if we had done so we would have seen no more of the Yankees. But it was clearly impossible to carry out my plans. Captain Green could not go any farther. I was very much afraid he would be seriously ill. I could not leave him. I determined therefore to go up to the nearest farm-house, get some restoratives for the Captain and if necessary put him to bed while I took to the woods in the vicinity and would visit him at night as I found opportunity. With this purpose we turned out of the main road into a lane or neighborhood road which, I afterwards learned, leads to Winnsboro. We had proceeded up this road about a quarter of a mile when Captain Green sat down on a pile of rails by the roadside, put his head down upon his knees, and declared that it was no use—he could not go any farther. "Wait here, Captain," said I. "I will be back in a moment." Leaving him here, I ran on as fast as I could.

Directed by the crowing of cocks in the early dawn, I turned through a gate which promised to lead to a farm-house. On I ran at full speed—it seemed to me that I should never reach it. On still I ran. Here it is at last, about half-a-mile from where I left Captain Green. I reached the house just at break of day—all is still as death. "Hello! Hello!! Hello!!!"—each time louder. A huge watchdog rushed towards me barking furiously, but was checked by the voice of a servant-girl. I asked to see her master or her mistress, and at the same time followed her to the house. At the door a woman met me whose expression of face I shall never forget. It was the picture of extreme terror, ghastly pale and such eyes! enormously large, opened to their widest stretch and one of them squinted until nothing but the white was visible. That ghastly terror-stricken face staring at me in the gray dawn will haunt me forever. Very soon she was joined by her husband who, mistaking me for a Yankee, had fled through the back door. The Yankees, they said, had a few of them been at their house the day before and had told the wife that they would return today in great numbers and would *"clean her out."* They were looking for them every moment and had mistaken me for an advance guard. I told my story and they kindly offered to do anything they could for the Captain even at some risk of suffering for their kindness. I therefore ran swiftly back to the place I had left Captain Green. He had gone.

Supposing I had gone straight up the road, after resting he had gone on. Suspecting this, I walked rapidly, sometimes running, and overtook him just before we reached another farm-house about half-a-mile farther, belonging to a Mr. Jones, immediately on the road. Here then we stopped and told our story. Mr. Jones was of course in the woods with the mules to save them, but Mrs. Jones received us hospitably. A few Yankees had visited her the day before and she also was momently expecting their return in great numbers.

It might be dangerous to remain in the house long, but it was absolutely necessary for us to take food, and possibly for Captain Green to take to his bed. She soon had ready for us a warm breakfast and a hot cup of rye-coffee. These luxuries together with a blazing fire seemed quickly and completely to restore the Captain. His meagre body and shrunk shanks seemed to absorb and actually to drink in the genial warmth and visibly to expand under its benign influence. While imbibing my coffee (so-called) I was surprised to learn that some one at the gate wished to see me, and still more surprised on going out to find a friend and fellow-townsman, Moultrie Gibbes. He was still more surprised to see me, for he had only heard from the hostess that there were two Confederates within. By rapid series of questions and answers we soon became acquainted with each other's situation. He had been a prisoner in the hands of the Yanks and was released yesterday on parole—had not seen John—had heard from Yankee officers that Columbia had been destroyed by fire—was on his way to Columbia, and would be there by night. We both hoped that the news of the burning of Columbia was exaggerated, or at least that the College buildings and therefore my home were probably spared, as these buildings were used as a hospital. I sent encouraging messages to our families—"Goodbye—goodbye, and tell my wife the Yanks shan't catch me."

On coming back to the house I found Captain Green in a most blissful state of mind. He was sitting before a blazing lightwood fire with his lank legs crossed one upon the other, his head thrown gently back and resting upon the top of his chair and enveloped in a cloud of tobacco-smoke as in a halo of glory, while his eyes languidly closed and again opened and gazed through the smoke upon the ceiling. I was deeply touched by the scene. It seemed holy as the sleep of childhood guarded by angels. I approached on tiptoe. Shall I break through the strong but gauzy veil woven about him by the magician Tobacco? Can I rudely bring back his soul from the heaven of Narcotism, tenanted only by good angels of peaceful and innocent thoughts, to the dull earth overrun by vile Yankees? Alas, it must be. Surrounded by dangers as we now are, is not he rather like Samson asleep in the lap of Delilah? "The Philistines be upon thee, Captain!" shouted I. In an instant he burst the magic chains that bound him and was ready for action. It was well there was no jawbone of an ass lying around loose, nor any Yankees in sight, or there is no telling what he might have attempted. "To the woods, then, as soon as possible," said I.

We started out for hiding-ground soon after sunrise. We were scarcely settled in a thick clump of pine saplings about half-a-mile from Mrs. Jones' when the popping of Yankee guns and the rising columns from burning homesteads proclaimed the arrival of the enemy and the commencement of their daily work. As we were not near any house we soon became indifferent, and tired nature began to assert itself. About 9 A.M., the sun having warmed us thoroughly, we became very sleepy. I proposed to watch while the Captain slept. He accordingly threw himself down in the sunniest place he could find and was soon snoring lustily. About 2 P.M. he awoke and we ate our lunch of cold boiled pork and stale cornbread. Then Captain Green watched while I slept. Thus the day passed away without any remarkable incident.

A welcome pipe.

As night approached and the popping of guns had ceased, the question, How shall we pass the night? began to press seriously upon us. Captain Green declared that another such night as the last would certainly kill him. We could not stay at night at a farm-house because, although we did not believe there was much personal risk in so doing, inasmuch as we had observed that the Yankees did not prowl about very much at night, yet we might bring distress and loss upon the hospitable owner for harboring us. We concluded therefore that we would spend the night at one of the numerous fires which we saw burning in every direction around us. It was necessary, however, first to learn as much as possible about the movements of the Yankees— what road they would take when they moved, etc.

With this determination, soon after dark we took our way back to Mrs. Jones' through the thick woods.

"Doctor, don't you hear two persons talking together behind us? I think someone is following us." We stopped, listened. "I think I hear it too," said I, "but I believe it is all imagination." On we went. When within fifty yards of Mrs. Jones' house, we secreted ourselves behind a fence and matured our plans. "Wait here, Captain," said I. "I will approach and reconnoitre to see if there are any Yankees in the house" (for Mrs. Jones' was a kind of public house). In case there were any Yankees there the danger was that dogs might betray us. I therefore approached with great caution, gliding silently but swiftly from one ornamental bush in the yard to another. When within ten steps of the door, I heard two persons coming rapidly along the road directly to the house. I slipped back quickly to the fence and waited until they passed—one was a white boy and the other a negro man. The boy went to the house, the man to the negro quarters. There were dogs at the negro cabins, but apparently none at the house.

I approached more boldly, and near to the door looked in. I saw a large number of persons sitting about the large open fireplace. Most of them sat with their backs to me, but Mrs. Jones sat near the farther corner with her face directly towards me and strongly illuminated by the fire. The company seemed to be neighbors gathered to discuss the events of the day. I listened some time. From Mrs. Jones' face and from the free tone of the conversation I concluded that none of the company were Yankees. At any rate, Mrs. Jones will see me first and will warn me. I therefore walked boldly and with distinct tread (in order to attract Mrs. Jones' attention) into the piazza and to the open door of the hall.

As I stood a moment at the door ready to enter, Mrs. Jones saw and instantly recognized me. Her whole countenance changed in a moment, and throwing up both her hands she exclaimed in a voice suppressed but full of terror, "My God! Don't come in here!" I remained standing stock-still. She jumped up and ran to me in the piazza. "What's the matter?" asked I. "Are there any Yankees with you?" "No," said she, "but they have just this moment left by the back door. They must be still in the yard. You are in great danger."

I told her I had come to learn the situation and would not leave until I had learned all I could. "Come this way, then, out of the light," said she, taking me into the front yard. She now told me that she gathered from the Yankees that their destination was Winnsboro—that the main body had gone through Allston, but several regiments had crossed Little river and would go to Winnsboro by this neighborhood road, which was a cut-off leading into the main road from Columbia to Winnsboro. They said, moreover, that they would be all gone from this vicinity by tomorrow night. This was good news. I then asked her about the fires I saw in every direction. "That," said she, "is a neighbor's house—that another neighbor's house—there you see are the embers of my cotton-house and all my cotton. My dwelling-house they did not burn; yonder fire is my burning fence, and that yonder is Mr. Leitner's." I left her, determined to spend the night at one of the burning fences.

I now went back to Captain Green, who was still where I left him in the fence-corner. I had been gone some time, half-an-hour or so. He was suffering very much from cold. We chose Leitner's fence as most suitable, and reached it about 9 P.M. The fence was burning splendidly on both sides of the road. We selected a spot where we would be partly sheltered from observation and near the ruins of a log cabin, behind which we might fly in case of danger. "Ah, Doctor," said the Captain as he squatted within three feet of the blazing fire, extended his long fingers and spread out his blanket-cloak so as to catch and reflect the heat upon his meagre body, "isn't this glorious?"

We had eaten nothing since breakfast except a slice or two of half-raw pork, nearly pure fat, and a crust of stale corn-bread as dry as sawdust—the same which was given us by the negroes on leaving camp last night. It was near 10 P.M. and we were very hungry. We broiled the re-mains of the pork and found it delicious. The cornbread was incapable of improve-

Leitner.

ment—we had to force it down the best way we could.

We had just finished our scanty meal, the Captain had just lit his much-loved pipe and was fumigating himself into Elysium, when the crushing of dry leaves under cautiously advancing footsteps caught our soon attentive ears. The footsteps had approached from the woods on the other side of the road and were close upon us before we were aware. We instantly retreated from the bright light of the fire into the darkness, but we had doubtless been observed while sitting at the fire. "Who goes there?" demanded a deep voice. "Who are you?" I asked in return. "I will know first who you are," returned the voice. "Friends from the woods," said I. "I am also from the woods," said he. "Confederates," said I. "All right," said he. *We* immediately came forward to the fire, and so did *he*. He was a stout, robust, weather-beaten man, clad in rough overcoat, home-made pants and heavy boots. He was very much excited and very violent in manner and language—oaths and curses poured forth from him in a continuous stream like lava from a volcano—curses against the Yankees, curses against the "niggers" and curses against his luck. We soon found that he was Leitner and I at once recognized him as the man whom I had frightened out of his own house at daybreak this morning. He said he had been in the woods about four miles off all day with his horses and mules—that he had left them in the care of two of his negro men and was now on his way home to see how the Yankees had served him—that seeing his fence afire he had stopped to arrest the flames, when on approaching he saw two persons who he supposed might be straggling Yankees. He had not yet been home to his family. After tearing down two or three panels, in which we heartily assisted him, and thus isolating the fire, he left us and went up to his house.

In about an hour he returned to us with a servant-girl (the same who had asked me to his house this morning), bringing a pot of hot rye-coffee with cups and saucers and a few warm biscuits. We greatly enjoyed his coffee and biscuits and were really grateful for his unexpected kindness. As she was leaving we asked the servant-girl if her mistress had any sweet potatoes—we would pay her well for them. She went back to the house and soon returned with a sack containing more than a peck, and said her mistress would take nothing in return. Leitner soon left us to return to his horses in the woods and we were again alone. We sat by the fire and roasted potatoes all night. By morning nearly all had somehow disappeared. The Captain declared and will always believe that most of them were lost among the ashes. Under this conviction he put on his spectacles and sought long and diligently for those lost potatoes, but in vain. But he is not convinced, his faith in his theory remains unshaken. "Eaten a peck of potatoes! Impossible—they are lost— what a pity," and he shook his head slowly and gravely.

Feb. 21st.—So soon as approaching morn began to "dapple the young East with spots of gray" we rose, shook ourselves, reluctantly left our now smouldering fire and started for the woods with the remaining raw potatoes tied up in our handkerchiefs. Our policy was never to use the same hiding place a second time, lest our return may have been observed by some prowling negro. We started therefore for a thicket which had been recommended by Leitner. The air was clear, crisp and bracing and the ground hard-frozen. It was really exhilarating. We soon found Leitner's thicket, but immediately rejected it as a hiding place. We had become connoisseurs in this matter. This one did not suit us at all— it was entirely *too* good—it would attract suspicion at once. Besides, there were already hidden there several waggons full of corn, and the waggon-tracks were visible running in all directions. We must find some other place. We tried another and better place, but this was too near a little hut from which we observed smoke rising. This was probably inhabited by some negro, [and] we must avoid observation. In the meantime the sun was up, the Yankee guns were already popping, and we were yet unconcealed. We flitted about like belated spectres from bush to bush, taking advantage in our rapid transit across open places now of a fence, then of a gully. Finally, about 9 A.M. we approached in our fearful rambles, without recognizing it, the main road to Columbia. We determined to cross this road and try a thicket which we saw crowning a hill on the other side. The woods near the road is a fine open forest of large oaks and entirely without underbrush. I advised Captain Green to lie down behind a log while I reconnoitred.

On reaching the fence and looking up the road I saw about a hundred yards distant a large number of negroes—men, women and children, coming rapidly towards me, with huge bundles, apparently bedding, on their heads. Immediately after I first perceived them they set down their bundles and rested. We have already been twice betrayed by negroes—we avoid them as carefully as we do Yankees. I immediately fell back to Captain Green and informed him of what I had seen. He agreed with me that it was best to remain where we were and let them pass before we crossed. The bundles were heavy, for they rested a half-hour. At the end of that time they passed on with their huge bundles four feet in diameter on their heads, and we crossed the road and the adjoining field unobserved and gained and approved the hiding place about ten A.M. A few still-remaining slices of half-raw pork, a few crumbs of sawdust corn-bread and an abundance of raw potatoes saved from last night formed our food for the day. No incident of any importance occurred. Judging by the firing of Yankee guns and the smoke of burning houses we think the Yankees are moving off towards Winnsboro. As on yesterday, so today we watched and slept alternately.

(NOTE: I learned afterwards that the laden company were our own negroes returning to Columbia. I did not dream of this at the time, or we would have been glad to have spoken to them and sent messages home. They were to have gone back yesterday, and we supposed them now at home.)

I have observed every day since I have been hiding from the Yankees a most singular phenomenon in my own person. It is the phenomenon of "imaginary conversations." It is well known that when the attention is stretched to the utmost limit, especially in the presence of undefined danger, the imagination often deceives us through the senses. The eye is the organ most commonly deceived in such cases.

> In the dark imagining some fear
> How easy is a bush supposed a bear.

But in my own case my eye played me no such fantastic tricks. I saw neither ghost nor bear nor imaginary Yankee. On the other hand, I could at any time by listening attentively *hear* two persons of differently pitched voices talking together in a low tone. On Sunday 19th, the day our waggons were captured, while in comparative security in the pine thicket on the north-east of our camp, I heard it very distinctly. It seemed to be two negroes conversing together. I was at the time extremely anxious about my brother John, and striving in vain to communicate with the negroes. I supposed it was some of our own negroes, perhaps scattered by fear of the Yankees and talking together in low, earnest voices. The peculiar accent of low-country negroes and the peculiar inflection of voice, easily detectable even when the words are not heard, was very distinct. So certain was

I, that I several times walked towards them and as they seemed to avoid me I even pursued them. It was like the benighted Athenian chasing the voice of Puck through the woods in "Midsummer Night's Dream." In fact, it is not improbable that the knowledge of the phenomenon I am now describing may have suggested this exquisite scene to the great dramatist. I did not mention this phenomenon before because I soon perceived that it was wholly imaginary and therefore was somewhat ashamed of it. Again on the same night, soon after the Yankee cavalry left us near Little river, the voices to which Capt. Green called my attention and which we took such pains to avoid were doubtless imaginary. Again during the whole day following, while [we were] lying concealed and especially while returning through the woods by night to Mrs. Jones', the same imaginary talking was distinct. I have heard it repeatedly today, in fact every time I listen attentively, but have learned to disregard it utterly.

Our stock of provisions is entirely exhausted, even to the last raw potato. We must get something to eat tonight, and a supply to last through tomorrow. At nightfall therefore we took our way back to Leitner's. "There may be Yankees there, Captain," said I; "who knows?" On approaching the house, therefore, Capt. Green remained about fifty yards distant, while I approached the gate and reconnoitred. Every door and window was closely shut and absolute silence reigned. I must call— "Hello, hello!" A negro girl came out (the same who brought the potatoes and who seems a most faithful creature to her mistress), silenced the barking of the house-dog, and ushered us into the house.

Mrs. Leitner received us with unaffected kindness—
she is not so hideous as yesterday in the grey dawn. She
cooked and then made us sit down to an excellent supper of fried bacon and hot cornbread and biscuit. Really
she is beginning to grow quite good-looking—her kind
woman's heart reveals itself in her face and beautifies it.
There has been but few Yankees about today, she says,
and thinks they are all gone on to Winnsboro this afternoon. She cordially invited us to stay at her house all
night. Mr. Leitner had not come in—we might be a protection to her—it would be no inconvenience, as she had
a spare room and a good bed. Thus her kind heart concealed itself behind a show of self-interest. Is not this
true politeness? Is not this a true gentlewoman—a lady?
With some hesitation lest we should bring trouble upon
her, we accepted her invitation.

Captain Green now thinks her real handsome. The
Yankees, she says, took away all her tobacco—she was
yearning for a smoke. The Captain gallantly offered her

Our hostess and Captain Green smoking, myself roasting potatoes.

his tobacco-bag. They each filled a pipe and smoked eternal friendship. In the meantime I squatted before the fire and roasted potatoes for our next day's provision in the woods. It was a sweet picture and carried my mind back to the peacefulness and the innocence of the olden time. I alternately turned my potatoes and watched the two in silent admiration. On the one side of the chimney sat Mrs. Leitner, leaning gently forward with her elbows on her knees, and puffing quietly in a peculiarly graceful and feminine manner, her eyes in the intensity of her enjoyment rolling and squinting and playing Bo-peep with each other—on the other sat the gallant Captain, his right hand supporting his pipe while his left hand supported the elbow of his right arm; from time to time darting a furtive glance across the way from under his bushy eyebrows, and then chuckling softly to himself with a gentle agitation of the diaphragm, a scarcely perceptible shaking of his gaunt sides and a slight showing of his canines. What is the meaning of his chuckling? Is it in anticipation of sleeping in a bed once more, or is it that he doubly enjoyed his pipe "on the lips of a friend?" Or does he mistake the meaning of Mrs. Leitner's squinting? I can't tell.

About 9 P.M. we bid our kind hostess good night, went to our room and without undressing threw ourselves on the bed. Oh, what a glorious bed! Of the soundness and deep dreamless forgetfulness of that sleep I knew nothing until next morning.

Feb. 22nd.—Mrs. Leitner, good careful soul, was up this morning by four o'clock preparing breakfast for her husband (who had come in late last night) and for ourselves in order that we might eat and be off by daybreak.

We chose for hiding-ground the same pine thicket which we had used for this purpose on Monday 20th. We reached it before sunrise. About 9 A.M. it commenced raining. Capt. Green decided it would kill him to get wet. So, as there seem to be very few Yankees about, we determined to strike southward for the small cabin which we had observed in our rambling yesterday—Mr. Leitner had told us this morning that it belonged to him and was occupied by an old negro woman who was entirely faithful. On the way, however, the rain having again stopped, and we having found a beautiful pine thicket, we concluded it was not worth while to go any further.

Our walk through the woods this morning revealed the somewhat startling fact that all the woods and the pine thickets in this vicinity had been searched by the Yankees on yesterday. The tracks of their horses were thickly scattered all over our hiding-ground and through those we had rejected yesterday. It was well for us that we crossed over the main road yesterday—I do not see how otherwise we could have escaped.

We hear very little firing today and see no smoke of burning houses. The few shots we hear we suspect are fired by boys or negroes. We therefore observe far less caution than heretofore. As the day is overcast and chilly and it has sprinkled several times, and as Captain Green suffers much from cold, we concluded we might with safety build a small fire of pine knots. This done, we warmed our feet and roasted our potatoes and remained comfortable all the afternoon.

Leitner visited us at our camp today, being guided thereto by the smoke of our fire. "This is what you call hiding, is it?" said he. "I don't believe there are any Yankees about," said I. "Don't you be too sure of that," said he. Leitner has small parcels of provisions hidden out all about in the woods. He is roaming about and examining these. Some are safe, some have been discovered and taken. He is restless and excited, cursing and swearing as usual. He talked with us for a few minutes in a violent manner, and was off again tearing frantically through the thickets to look after still other parcels of hidden provisions.

By urgent invitation of Leitner we took our way back to his house at nightfall. A blazing fire awaited us and welcomed our return. We all, except Leitner, concluded the Yankees were all gone and that we might safely go *towards* if not *to* Columbia tomorrow. But Leitner is restless and uneasy, haunted by imaginary terrors—terrors from Yankees, terrors from negroes; he is very unwilling that we should go. Meanwhile the fragrance of broiled bacon began to assail our nostrils and to excite our salivaries. The evening meal was on the table and we were just about to sit down, when one of the Leitner children, a girl of about eight years old, who had been looking out of the back door, cried out in alarm, "Oh, father! Look yonder!" We ran to the door and saw a house afire about half-a-mile off. All our hopes of starting to Columbia in the morning vanished in a moment. It was not even safe for us to stay in Leitner's house. The incendiaries could be none other than Yankees, and here they were roaming about at night contrary to their usual custom.

We hastened out immediately, determined to spend the night in the woods, for we would not bring trouble upon kind Mrs. Leitner. The latter ran out to us with a bowl of milk, which we drank, then crammed our pockets full of biscuits and cornbread. Thus fortified, we started towards the fire, munching our provisions as we went. Having reached the top of a high hill overlooking the burning building, we sat down and watched the fire until it sank in smouldering brands, but saw no Yankees. The house was well known, of course, to Leitner. Finding it rather dull watching thus in silence, Leitner and I lay down on the thick bed of dry leaves while Captain sat and smoked his beloved pipe. In a few minutes we were fast asleep. About twelve o'clock Capt. Green awakened us. The fire had gone down. Everything was still as death.

We went back to Leitner's house, sat up till one o'clock, and, there being no further signs of Yankees, went to bed.

Feb. 23rd.—Off again by daybreak to yesterday's hiding place. We might, we think, start this morning in safety for Columbia, but Leitner is so anxious for us to remain with him until things are quieter. We prefer, too, not to start until we are sure of the passage through, for we are not likely to meet again such kind friends as the Leitners. Our provision today consisted of cold slices of fried bacon, cornbread and potatoes both roasted and raw. Captain Green is greatly astonished at the quantity of raw sweet potatoes which I daily consume. Poor fellow, he is dyspeptic—I find them both palatable and wholesome.

It is still cloudy and chilly today with occasional slight sprinklings of rain. We therefore kept up a small fire all day. No popping of Yankee guns or burning of

Confederate houses nor any other evidence of the presence of the enemy today to enliven us. We therefore relieved the tedium by discussing Poetry, the Drama, Science and Philosophy. In the intervals of the discussion of these high questions we munched roasted potatoes.

Leitner came to our camp today and told us that he had ascertained from several sources that the incendiaries of last night were seven Yankee stragglers—that they had remained all night in a negro cabin in the vicinity of the burned building, and had gone on towards Winnsboro this morning.

At night we went back as usual to Leitner's house. We have made friends of all the children, the servants, the dogs and the cats about the house. They all greet us kindly on our return, each in his several way—with smiles or tail-wagging or gentle purrings and rubbings against our legs.

On our way to the house tonight Leitner overtook us, and told us in a hoarse whispering voice which trembled with alarm that a negro man belonging to Dr. LaBorde had threatened his life. Leitner it seems had been very severe with this negro, who was a notorious rascal. He had once flogged him and once shot at him for stealing his hogs. We tried to reason with him and show him the absurdity of his fears, but all in vain. He looked upon himself, he said, as a "doomed man." When he reached home he took his little crippled boy—a quiet, affectionate, intelligent fellow of twelve years who was suffering with spinal disease—on his knee, folded him in his arms, kissed him affectionately and told him with the utmost seriousness and apparent deep feeling that he expected to be murdered, and that when he was gone he [the boy] must take care of his mother, his little brothers and sisters. It was difficult to suppress a smile while this tragicomedy was going on. His wife reproached him, though kindly, for his idle fears. We paid no attention to his gloom but talked cheerfully on indifferent matters, and gradually he became more cheerful also. The supper was smoking on the table—our appetites were already whetted to the keenest edge by the rising fragrance—we had taken our seats—I had just raised my fork and held it poised in mid-air ready to plunge it into the heart of a most tempting piece of fried bacon, when the servant Margaret opened the door and said, "Somebody at de gate say, *hello*." In an instant Leitner, the Captain and myself were out of the back door and over the rail fence. Here we stopped and listened. We heard first the voices of several men, then footsteps approaching the house, then the tramp of at least three pairs of heavy boots on the piazza, then the same in the hall—alas, for our supper—then the back door opened—alas, for ourselves, they are upon us. We had just prepared ourselves for a precipitate retreat, when instead of the wild yell of Yankees we heard in gentle feminine accents, "Henry! Henry!" It was Mrs. Leitner calling her husband—this was of course the signal that all was right.

On coming to the house we found there three Confederates belonging to the medical department, fugitives from before the face of Sherman and now making their way back to Columbia. They had walked today from Newberry and had met many pedestrians from Columbia who all concurred in stating that there were no Yankees there nor on the way. Oh, joyful news! Hurrah for Columbia in the morning—rain or shine, storm or fair,

I will sleep at home tomorrow night. "If I have a home to sleep in!" Ah, me! how that "if" chilled my joy. But we will hope for the best. Upon further inquiry our new acquaintances informed us that they were told that four-fifths of Columbia was burned, but that the College buildings were probably spared—yes, yes, I will hope for the best. We ate our supper in an ecstasy of spirits. Leitner alone seemed gloomy and downcast. He was very unwilling for us to go—begged that the Captain at least would stay with him—Captain was feeble—it was threatening a storm—Captain ought not to go in bad weather. He was evidently still brooding over the threat of LaBorde's negro man.

My almost childish impatience for the morrow kept me awake some time after retiring. At last I sank into a deep sleep and dreamed of home.

Feb. 24th.—Raining in torrents this morning—Capt. Green is doubtful about going. He cannot walk the whole distance of twenty miles in one day. Leitner urged him to stay. The Captain's revolver had great excellences in his eyes. After much hesitation the Captain decided to go at least a part of the way with us. Poor Leitner is inconsolable. He went immediately to the woods and brought thence all his guns, double-barrelled, single-barrelled, rifles, cleaned them thoroughly, loaded them heavily, and then declared himself ready for the d———d nigger.

After a hearty breakfast and a still more hearty good-bye to our kind hostess, who could not be induced to take a cent in return for all her kindnesses, a hearty goodbye to Margaret the faithful servant, and to all the children, a head-patting for old Caesar the watch-dog and a back-stroking for Pussy, we started off in high spirits, Leitner accompanying with two guns, one on each shoulder. The other guns he left with his crippled eldest boy with the parting injunction that he should use them in defence of the family. Leitner promised that he would take us a short cut through the woods which would lessen the distance about two miles and would take us by his horses and mules. They had had, he said, neither food nor water for four days. Onward we went across fields, through woods—straight over hill and down dale and across streams—"through bush and through briar," splashing along "through dub and mire"—Leitner seemed actually afraid of the road. At last we reached Leitner's horses and found them doing as well as could be expected. Leitner took them along, and we came out on the main road at Dr. Turnipseed's. Instead of gaining anything by Leitner's short cut, we had lost much both in time and distance and still more in strength. The truth is, he was afraid of going after his horses and mules without our company. We had suspected this at first, but his kindness required that we should humor him even at considerable personal inconvenience.

At Dr. Turnipseed's, Leitner was again thrown into an ecstasy of alarm and again begged us not to leave him. The circumstances were these. We found Dr. Turnipseed's family on our arrival in a state of great excitement. They had sent a negro man in a buggy with a considerable quantity of bacon with instructions to give it to a relative who had been robbed of all his provisions by the Yankees. In a very few moments the negro returned on foot saying that two men in *blue* who said they were Yankees had met him but a little way from the house, had violently taken away buggy, horse, bacon and all and driven off towards Columbia. They must, we supposed, be stragglers. Two stragglers cannot harm us—we are four. We determined to push on in spite of stragglers. With a rueful face Leitner bade us goodbye, and on we went.

It was now 10 A.M. and only fifteen miles to Columbia. I can easily get home to supper, thought I. On we went, then, at a swinging gait, my heart beating higher with the hope of taking supper at home this evening. Captain Green did his best to keep up with us, but in vain. I tried my best to control my impatience and walk slower for his sake, but I could not. I found it easier to stop entirely than to control my pace. At the top of every hill I was compelled to stop while Captain Green's tall spare form with his blanket-coat around his shoulders and his hood drawn closely over his head toiled slowly and steadily along. The rain poured in torrents—the creeks and swamps were all flooded—no matter—on we plunged without a moment's hesitation, often through water to the middle of the thigh. As I press on from time to time I glance down at my dilapidated clothing. Alas, how can I appear at home among friends—among ladies—in the streets of Columbia in such garb? My shirt and underclothes I have had on now nearly two weeks, and I have no others even when I get home. Worst of all

> My *galligaskins* that have long withstood
> The winter's fury and encroaching frosts
> By Time subdued (what will not Time subdue?)
> An *horrid chasm* disclose....

But it can't be helped, so onward we press at [a] still increasing rate.

Thus we "skelpit on thro' dub and mire" until about half-past one P.M. We were all very hungry—Captain was not only hungry but he was completely exhausted. He must have food, he must have rest. At a venture I went up to a respectable-looking house and knocked. When the door opened I was surprised to find friends, refugees from Columbia and Charleston—the Rev. Mr. Wilson from Columbia and Dr. Frost* and family from Charleston. I received the heartiest of welcomes—"Come in, come in and bring your friends, take dinner with us and stay all night." I replied that I could not stay except for dinner, but that Captain was feeble and exhausted and I would be glad if they would entertain him until tomorrow. "Certainly, certainly." In a moment the Captain was shown to a room and soon reappeared looking really regal in his dry clean clothes—think of it—clean shirt, white stockings, gorgeously flowered slippers and

* The Rev. Dr. Robert Wilson, rector of St. Luke's church (Episcopal), Charleston, who was at this time in Columbia with his father-in-law, the Rev. Dr. Peter J. Shand, rector of Trinity church (Episcopal), Columbia; and Dr. Francis LeJau Frost, a physician of Charleston.

Dr. Wilson had been a physician before he became a clergyman. Major Green was also a physician. It is to be noted, then, that when the clergyman, the soldier, the doctor, and the chemist met under the same roof, it was a meeting of four men of medicine.

Dr. Frost, fleeing as a refugee from Charleston, left one of the finest of the old Charleston residences, the "Pringle house" (his wife had been Miss Susan Pringle), at No. 27 King Street. This house, which in colonial days had been the first American home of Lord William Campbell, the last British governor of South Carolina, was soon to become the headquarters of the Federal general, John P. Hatch, who at the end of the war was placed in command of the Military District of Charleston, the chief one of the several districts into which the State was divided for purposes of military administration.

splendid dressing-gown. He could not have been prouder
if he had been arrayed in purple and fine linen.

I then asked concerning Columbia. "Almost entirely
consumed." "The College buildings?" asked I. "They are
spared." "Thank God, I have a home still." Dinner was
then announced, and such a dinner! Sherman had not
come so far up this road; they had everything that heart
could dream or stomach crave, and coffee too! Real genuine coffee! I have not tasted any for two years—A-a-a-h!
how delicious!

About half-past three P.M. we are ready to start again.
Captain in his imperial dressing-gown is reclining in a
large easy-chair, his head thrown back and resting on
its deep cushion, his feet encased in gorgeous slippers
resting on the fender, his pants slightly drawn up so
as to show the snow-white stockings which encased his
meagre shanks, his classic head encircled with a beautiful halo of tobacco smoke, and such a heavenly look of
happiness and content on his noble face. I again com-
mend him to their kindness and bade my kind friends
goodbye. "Shall I tell your wife and daughter that you
will be with them tomorrow, Captain?" Without chang-
ing in the least his position but only languidly opening
his eyes, he replied, "Yes—yes, I will be there tomorrow."
"Goodbye"—and away we went again. On, on we strode
at a still increasing rate, my strength braced by the good
dinner, by the splendid coffee, the warm kindness we
had just received, but more, much more, than all by the
certainty now that I would sup with my family. Only
six miles! I will walk that in an hour and a half. And
I did. I stepped out with increasing vigor. One of my
companions had a heavy carpet-bag to carry. He remon-

strated—it was impossible, he said, for him to keep up. "Give me the carpet-bag; come on," I said. I took the bag, slung it across my shoulders, and on we strode at [a] still increasing rate.

We entered Columbia at the extreme northern end (Cottontown) and went down the whole length of Main Street for a mile and a half. Not a house remaining. Only the tall chimneys standing gaunt and spectral, and empty brick walls with vacant windows like death-heads with eyeless sockets. The fire had swept five or six blocks wide right through the heart of the city. Only the eastern and western outskirts are left. We met not a living soul—"Alas, how the beautiful city, the Pride of the State, sits desolate and in ashes!" But I have no time to moralize now—onward still with increasing speed—yonder see the brick walls of the campus and the buildings of the College, and see, there at last is my own ivy-covered home! I resigned the carpet-bag to my companion, who takes rooms in the hospital, ran up the tall stone steps three at a leap. Door locked. Rap! Rap!! Rap!!! Loud, sharp, quick. Deep silence a moment—then the quick pattering of little feet along the hall—then in an instant open flew the door and they all hung upon my neck with mingled laughter and tears.

"Oh, father, you are soaking wet!" said one. "Oh, papa! you are in rags—your pants are hanging in strings about your feet, and look! what a rent on one knee!" "Yes, my daughter, and I am afraid there are much bigger ones hidden beneath my coat-tails." "Do go and change your clothes." "My daughter, I have none but these." "Oh, I forgot. What *will* you do?" "We'll see about that in good time. I suppose you heard of the capture of the waggons, the loss of everything—the carrying off of John, and my life in the woods?" "Yes, yes, Sandy told us all about it, but oh, we are so glad the Yankees didn't catch you."

It seems they all were congratulating themselves that we had escaped with the baggage when Sandy returned on Tuesday and told the whole dreadful story. All were in great distress for the loss of so much valuable property, much of it of tenfold more value through association, but in much more distress, in an agony of anxiety, for our personal safety. We might be shot as bushwhackers, they feared. Sandy only laughed at these fears—"Yah, yah, yah! You needn't trouble yourself, Missis—dem Yankee nebber ketch Mossa—dat sartain shore." Johnny came back the same day (21st or 22nd), having been released by the Yankees, and confirmed Sandy's story.

Then followed the recital of experiences on either side. Mine I have already given, but theirs—ah, theirs was far more dreadful. The terrors of the bombardment of the 16th and the morning of the 17th—the still greater terrors of the entrance and the occupation of the Yankee army—and the indescribable, the inconceivable horrors of the night of the 17th.

The College buildings, in spite of the guard, were set on fire several times and were only saved by the exertions of the physicians of the hospital. (The College campus is surrounded by a wall eight feet high in which there is but one opening, where a guard was placed by Sherman because the buildings were used as a hospital for soldiers of both sides.) At one time the destruction of the whole College seemed so certain that the patients were all moved out into the open area in the middle of the campus, and more than twenty of them died next day in consequence of exposure and fright. Several attempts to set my brother's house a-fire were only thwarted by constant watchfulness. At one time Mrs. LeConte thought our home was certainly gone. With the assistance of my faithful man-servant Henry she moved all the most valuable things into the back garden at some distance from the house, and then, taking up the baby (Carrie), wrapped her warmly in a blanket and carried her in her arms fast asleep out of the house far into the back garden, where she and all the children remained a considerable portion of the dreadful night.

"And did no one enter our house?" asked I. "Not a Yankee crossed the threshold of the door."—Ah, me! What a fatality seems to have pursued us and our waggons. If we had left the things at home they would have been safe. If we had remained where we camped the first night we would have been safe. If we had stopped with Rhett near the fourteen-mile house we would have been safe, for *he* saved his waggons, his man-servants, his maid-servants, his ox and his ass, his hogs and his turkeys. If we had stopped anywhere from three miles out of Columbia to within two or three miles of Little river we would have been safe. Finally, if we had on first starting come back to Columbia and taken the direct Allston road we would have been safe, for we would have passed Allston before Jeff. Davis'* corps reached there. This was what our friend Mr. Chas. Davis expected and therefore he urged our immediate departure—we were two full days going twenty miles, and all through taking the wrong road at first.

* Maj. Gen. Jefferson C. Davis, one of Sherman's corps commanders.

"By-the-way, what became of Mr. Davis?" I asked. Mr. Davis, I was told, on the night I left (the 15th) slept in our house, in my study in the basement. On being carried by Mrs. LeConte to the room, he examined carefully the doors and windows—saw that he could easily jump out in case of danger either into the front yard or else by another window into a side garden, opening by a gate into the back yard. He had been many nights, he said, with little sleep—he might sleep deeply—he begged that if there was any unusual noise he might be awakened promptly. He slept late next morning and went out after breakfast. During that day, 16th, he was arrested as a Yankee spy, the information being furnished by a negro woman belonging to Dr. Gibbes, but he was quickly recognized by several of our officers as one of our most trusted spies, and therefore released. That same night he came to John's house accompanied by a tall, dark, villainous-looking man (no doubt a Yankee spy), told the man to take notice of the house so that he would not mistake, and then told him in authoritative voice, "Remember, *I* protect this house." Next morning (17th), as the last Confederates were leaving the city, he came again to my house with some little trifles in his hand, ribbons, feathers etc., which he said he had picked up in the streets and which he begged my daughter Emma to accept as a memento of him, and saying— "Goodbye, I must leave, our army is going. If the Yankees enter your house I shall certainly be with them. Be sure you do not betray me by recognition"—he went and we never saw him more. Is he a Yankee spy? Or is he a spy on both sides? He is a greater mystery than ever.

Two weeks later.—Capt. Green came down to Columbia according to his promise the next day after my arrival (i.e., the 25th). He talks often of the good times he had at Dr. Frost's and especially of *that dressing-gown* and *those slippers*. John came back in about ten days. He had been carried to the borders of North Carolina and there released. He was compelled to walk all the way while a prisoner and much of the way on his return to Columbia, and arrived looking haggard and worn. For myself, my life in the woods agreed with me astonishingly—I was never heartier in my life.

Index